Endorsements

Carlos does a masterful job of weaving his journey into virtuous "lessons learned" that provide a road map on how to embrace life and focus on what is most important: faith, family, and the will to never, ever give up. Wonderful chapter quotes, and to that I would add, his story is embodied by the final sentence in Calvin Coolidge's famous quote, "Persistence and determination alone are omnipotent."

—Mac Curtis, former CEO and Chairman,
Perspecta (NYSE: PRSP)

A truly inspirational story of a dreamer and how he found his dream in a land that so many other dreamers and doers find theirs.

—Jim Mainor, Amway Diamond

I've known Carlos for thirty years, and I've had a front-row seat to much of what he writes here. His story is compelling: a young immigrant kid tackling the local bully on the streets of Newark, New Jersey; gaining admission to the prestigious Virginia Military Institute (despite a rejection letter!); driving limousines on the streets of Palm Beach; and finally, building a world-class cyber security business. Carlos has dreamed the dream and built the dream! What he says in this book will inspire you and motivate you to dream BIG and act on your dreams.

—Mark Murnan, Pastor,
Cornerstone Presbyterian Church,
Palm Beach Gardens, FL

For the past twenty years, Carlos has been a true friend—one who invests in and believes in me. Carlos's passion and authentic integrity inspire me to live life forward with enthusiasm and generosity. As I read *The Big Idea*, I found myself smiling with my friend's can-do attitude and humor as he shares a journey that we all can relate to. The Big Idea is chock full of inspiring nuggets and practical tools to realize your own potential. In this book, Carlos is the friend who comes alongside you and says, "Let's make your dream a reality."

—Timothy Chambers, Author and Artist,
featured in *The New York Times* best-selling books

I congratulate Carlos on this book, which is, above all, a written testimony of his journey where his perseverance, fueled by the dreams he believes in, has propelled him on his path to success, which he has based on fundamental values that have allowed him to create strong bonds of trust around him, always focused on a purpose that transforms and generates value for society. An excellent gift to society.

—António Gameiro Marques, Rear Admiral,
National Security Authority, Portugal

Carlos did an excellent job of incorporating many of his life experiences with timeless principles. He beautifully demonstrated how we all have the fight within us to overcome any challenges or struggles life throws us. That regardless of where we are at in life, we can dig deeper and find the strength and resolve to overcome and change our destiny. This book is a must read!

—Dave Doodnauth, Amway Diamond

As a first-generation Portuguese/American immigrant myself, I thoroughly enjoyed reading *The Big Idea* by Carlos Fernandes. His story is my story and also the story of many first-generation immigrants. The insights and school of hard knocks learnings Carlos shares in his book are golden pieces of information and guidance for any aspiring entrepreneur. A must read!

—Jorge Lopes, ACS Cyber SEAL

THE BIG
idea

**7 PRINCIPLES THAT WILL MOVE YOU
FROM A DREAMER TO A DOER**

CARLOS FERNANDES

FREILING
AGENCY

Published by Freiling Agency, LLC.

P.O. Box 1264
Warrenton, VA 20188

www.FreilingAgency.com

PB ISBN: 979-8-9888007-4-3
eBook ISBN: 979-8-9888007-5-0

Printed in the United States of America

Contents

Foreword

When I look back on my childhood, I see my father patiently and sometimes impatiently urging me to look for things to become passionate about. I remember at the age of four beginning to play soccer. My dad was the coach and he coached me for most of my soccer career. If he lacked something as a coach, he sought out other coaches to come in and train the team. He grew close to one coach in particular, Zik Jabar, and when my father decided to move on from coaching, many of the kids he coached as I grew up ended up going to Jabar's team.

A goal of mine had always been to make it onto his team, but I had yet to prove that I was capable of doing so. I remember finally making the team going into my sophomore year of high school after attempting to earn a spot for years prior and being denied. This passion of mine lasted until the beginning of my senior year, when many of my teammates had decided to either stop playing soccer or tried out for other teams.

Unsure of what to do next, I looked to my father for help and he suggested I give running a try. His reasoning was that since I was scrawny and looked like a runner, I'd probably excel in it. He was right. Seven years later, I'm still running. I even moved out west to Boulder, CO, to continue to pursue running at the highest level, desiring to see how good I can become.

That's the power of a BIG idea. He shared it with me and it grew bigger than each of us probably thought it would when we started. My father has always been a believer in others and selflessly wishes to encourage everyone he meets to pursue something they're passionate about—not just pursue, but find purpose in a passion that leads to purposeful living.

I hope that as you read this book, you become inspired as I have, and still am, by my father.

Here's to pursuing your BIG ideas!

—Carlos Fernandes II

Acknowledgments

I want to acknowledge the following people for the profound difference they have made in my life, and through it, they have made important contributions to this book.

Rafael Duarte Fernandes (dad) - deceased, March 11, 2017

Zelia Fernandes (mom)

Carminda Valente Fernandes (spouse)

Carlos Alberto Fernandes II (oldest son)

Cristina Victoria Fernandes (oldest daughter)

Catherine Isabella Fernandes (daughter)

Christopher Alexander Fernandes (son)

Costa Panais, a childhood friend, and lifelong friend for over 40 years (deceased).

Carlos dos Santos, a childhood friend, my first friend shortly after I arrived in the United States in the summer of 1974 (deceased).

Paul W. Pendorf II, one of my best friends since 1984. He encouraged me to go attend VMI.

COL Buchanan, former VMI Director of Admissions (deceased).

COL George Piegari, former head of the VMI Math and Computer Science Department. He saw potential in me that I did not see in myself at the time (deceased).

Bill Britt. Founder of the Britt Worldwide Organization, Amway Crown Ambassador. He shared the message of salvation with me in the Summer of 1992 that changed my life in ways that I cannot adequately communicate with words (deceased).

Anthony Infantini, I consider him as one of my best friends of almost 40 years.

Mark Murnan, a friend of over 30 years, pastor of a small church in Palm Beach County, FL.

Jack Gill, the Senior Pastor at Blue Ridge Bible Church, my pastor for 20 years.

Timothy Chambers, portrait artist, friend of 20 years.

Also, three dear family friends that died within the past year:

Gloria Baer, a neighbor and member of our local church family.

Olga Garber, a member of our local church family.

Megan Miller, wife of Brian Miller. Friends of over 20 years.

"Do you harbor a grand idea that ignites a spark within you, compelling you to stay awake at night?"

Introduction

In the bustling suburbs of Washington, D.C., where the world of cybersecurity takes center stage, Agile Cybersecurity Solutions (ACS) stands tall as one of America's leading companies, safeguarding networks for both commercial and government entities. As the founder and CEO of ACS, I am honored to be a trusted partner in the fight against hackers and the protection of the United States and its thriving businesses. It's a role I embrace with pride and gratitude, recognizing the hand of providence that led me here.

My journey, chronicled in this book, has been anything but ordinary. It's a tale of triumph over challenges and burdens that at times seemed insurmountable. Yet, with unwavering determination, I have conquered them, and my continued success stands as a testament to the power of perseverance and BIG ideas. I say this with humility, fully acknowledging that without the guiding hand of God, my story could have taken a vastly different turn.

As I pen these words, I find myself drawn back to the neighborhood of my birthplace, Portugal. Today, Portugal is ripe with opportunities for entrepreneurs like myself to flourish. While it may have more bureaucracy and socialism compared to the American business landscape, it has evolved into a more pro-business haven, vastly different from its earlier days. And thus, my journey in this book begins in the enchanting city of Lisbon where I write and do business.

Situated among seven picturesque hills, Lisbon is a charming port city on the Tagus River estuary, proudly holding the distinction of being the westernmost European capital. Its streets are adorned with pastel-colored buildings, showcasing elaborate architecture that weaves a mesmerizing tale of history and culture. Venture beyond its vibrant streets, and you'll find yourself immersed in medieval villages and sun-kissed stretches of sandy beaches, a paradise for those seeking peace and tranquility.

Lisbon's Mediterranean climate blesses most of the year with mild temperatures, while summers invite throngs of people to its shores to bask in the warm embrace of the sun. This city, once a hidden gem, now beckons travelers from far and wide, enchanting them with its allure. A paradise, some will say.

However, for my parents, Portugal was far from a paradise. In the 1960s, the country languished under the oppressive grip of a cooperative dictatorship known as the Estado Novo. Despite masquerading as a democracy, political freedoms were ruthlessly suppressed, leaving no room for progress or self-improvement. While not officially communism, it might as well have been, as countless individuals like my parents were trapped in the suffocating clutches of poverty and hopelessness.

Yet, even in the midst of despair, my father's resilience refused to be quelled. Faced with seemingly insurmountable odds, he resolved to craft an escape plan, a lifeline to a better future for his family. Though I was just a young boy at the time and memories are hazy, I distinctly recall the morning when my mother packed our suitcases, and we embarked on a journey to the airport. Our destination: America, where my father had already set out in search of new opportunities. As we embarked on that long flight, I knew little of the red, white, and blue that awaited us. However, upon landing in New York City, I beheld a sight that left an indelible mark on my heart—the Statue of Liberty. To me, she symbolized more than a grand monument; she embodied hope—the kind of hope that insists, despite all evidence to the contrary, that something greater and brighter lies just beyond the horizon.

Upon our arrival, we possessed nothing but hope—the first glimmer of its warmth in our lives. Hope, that powerful force residing within each of us, urged us forward, propelling us toward the possibilities and ideas that awaited. And indeed, those possibilities proved to be true. As immigrants to this great nation, my family and I are forever grateful for the opportunities it offered, granting us a new life filled with the promise of liberty and happiness. America, with its generous embrace, provided us the chance to rebuild, to strive, and to create a life that transcended the limitations of our past. It granted us the privilege to pursue our dreams and aspirations, unfettered by the shackles of poverty and oppression.

Today, as I stand on the precipice of nearly five decades since the adventure across the ocean that altered the course of my life, I find myself overwhelmed with gratitude. As I reflect on that little boy who emerged from the clutches of poverty in a distant land, now standing here, transformed by the relentless pursuit of opportunity and the blessings of freedom in America.

When you delve into the pages of my book, I hope you, too, will be moved to action on your big ideas. My story, when shared with others, often elicits incredulous expressions, as if it were a tale spun from the realm of fiction. But I assure you, it is as real as the air we breathe! From my escape from Portugal to the dark and dangerous streets of New Jersey where I fend for myself as a young boy, to the hot and humid coast of Florida where I discovered what it meant to be an

American and an entrepreneur, to one of the country's leading military institutes where I was educated and grew in strength and stature, to the United States military where I became disciplined, and finally through a maze of my big business ideas where I eventually landed in Washington, D.C., to found and lead my company, a trusted leader in cybersecurity. This book might be the culmination of my story, but not the end.

But this book is more than a mere memoir; it is a roadmap for aspiring entrepreneurs and business leaders like you, who seek to craft a better life for themselves and their families. As you begin to read, my desire is that you will prepare yourself for invaluable life lessons that will propel you toward success, regardless of your background or circumstances. Within these pages lie pearls of wisdom applicable to anyone, regardless of their situation. However, my mission is specifically meant to empower entrepreneurs and business leaders, like you, to dare to dream big and seize the extraordinary opportunities that await.

Do you harbor a grand idea that ignites a spark within you, compelling you to stay awake at night? Hold onto that idea, for it possesses the power to guide you toward an extraordinary future. Think of Jeff Bezos, who envisioned "the world's biggest bookstore." At first, skeptics abounded, yet today, we are all Amazon Prime members. And I've always loved the sage words of Henry Ford, "Whether you think you can, or think you can't—you're right." Indeed he was right as well and, in fact, we all drive his automobiles. Likewise, Jack Welch dreamed of making GE "the world's most competitive enterprise," and he succeeded through unwavering dedication and a revolutionary mindset. They all had big ideas and lived to see them come true.

Throughout my life, I have been told that I possess big ideas as well, and in these pages, you will discover how to embrace and manifest your own. This book serves as a testament that anyone, from any corner of the world, equipped with nothing more than determination, can ascend to greatness in the capital of the free world and beyond.

Prepare yourself to embrace the principles that will shape your journey:

- Refuse to be a victim or feel entitled, for empowerment lies in your hands.

- Cultivate an insatiable thirst for knowledge and continuous learning.

- Fixate on your endgame, for a clear vision fuels your path to triumph.

- Let financial constraints be mere obstacles that ignite your creativity and resourcefulness.

- Recruit a loyal and trustworthy team that will fortify your endeavors.

- Face adversity with courage, thriving even when your back is against the wall.

- Unleash your spirit and liberate your mind, unleashing the power of your big idea.

As you dive deeper into my story, embrace the essence of the Algarve that inspired me to dream big. With determination and action, you can transform your dreams into reality. Yes, let's remember the wisdom of T. Boone Pickens, "A plan without action is not a plan. It's a speech."

So, my friend, fasten your seatbelt. Let the stories shared here propel you to unlock the brilliance within as you pave your path to successful entrepreneur, fearlessly embracing your big ideas and creating your legacy. Let us both venture forth, for the future beckons and destiny awaits. It's time to stop dreaming and take action on your big ideas!

"When we face our problems
head-on, we awaken a
powerful force within us—
the force of resilience
and tenacity."

1

Perseverance Leads to Hope

Author John Connolly once wrote, "For in every adult there dwells the child that was, and in every child there lies the adult that will be." I'd say I agree with that. One of the luckiest things that can happen to you in life is, I think, to have a happy childhood. A happy childhood filled with laughter, love, and cherished memories, lays the groundwork for a lifetime of contentment. But the opposite does not necessarily have to be true.

Let me reveal a profound truth that I, along with many other immigrants, have learned. A tough childhood does not necessarily herald an unhappy adult. Too often in life we witness hearts burdened by the weight of blaming their present misfortunes on the past. It can be so enticing to place blame on our upbringing for the adversities we face today. Let me challenge you to embrace a different path, a path of empowerment and courage. For within each of us resides the potential to rise above the tribulations of the past and be the architects of our own fate.

Did I have a joyful childhood? Not necessarily, as you will soon learn. But I believe that my past suffering produced my present perseverance; perseverance, character; and character, hope. I decided early on in my life that I would be the author of my own saga, not my circumstances. So I fought my way through the negativity and became an eternal optimist. I want to see you do the same. Embrace the gift of hope, for in this very moment as you read this book, you have the power to persevere as well, penning your own story of triumph and inspiration for generations to come, no matter your upbringing.

Coming to America

When we first arrived in America, my father took my family across the river from New York to New Jersey where we settled. Jon Bon Jovi once said, "Heaven looks a lot like New Jersey." I tend to disagree! The State's motto is "Liberty and Prosperity," but in the 1970s there wasn't much of either. The 1970s was marked by significant social, cultural, and political transformation for New Jersey. In terms of demographics, New Jersey was becoming more diverse, with an influx of African American, Latino, and Asian immigrants. It was also a time of political activism, with many Jersey residents participating in protests and demonstrations on a variety of issues, including civil rights, the Vietnam War, and environmental concerns. The state's economy was transitioning from a reliance on manufacturing to a more service-oriented economy, and many Jersey towns were experiencing suburbanization and gentrification. Additionally, the state saw a rise in organized crime, which had a significant impact on urban areas.

It was a tough place to live, and this is where I spent my childhood. In the heart of New Jersey's gritty urban landscape, amidst the towering concrete jungles and bustling streets, laid the reality of life for a child. The vivid colors of childhood were painted against a backdrop of violence, offering both moments of resilience and the weight of hardship. My playground was a maze of alleyways and street corners where laughter echoes alongside the sounds of sirens and car horns. Play is a respite from the challenges that surround children. Yet, for me, even in play, the shadows of struggle lingered. The dilapidated buildings with boarded-up windows, a stark reminder of the economic hardships faced by the families who lived there.

The constant awareness of violence that permeated the air shaped my innocence into a cautious vigilance. I witnessed the repercussions of gangs, drugs, and crime. I learned to distinguish the pops of fireworks from the sound of gunshots. My young mind grappled with the harsh realities of life and death. It was amidst this life that I came face to face with the reality that I could either accept my doomed fate, or fight back and learn to rise above it.

Learning to Fight Back

When I was about ten years old, a young neighborhood boy named Richard Tory cast a dark shadow over the lives of those who crossed his path. He was a hulking figure, a bully who relished in his position of power and dominance on the streets. His very presence instilled fear in my friends and me, and his malevolence seemed to know no bounds.

One fateful day, destiny's hand led me into an unfortunate rendezvous with Richard. On this day, he decided that I was going to be his victim. He chased me through the streets as sweat trickled down my forehead, my heart pounded like a war drum, for I knew all too well the fate that awaited me. Richard, the embodiment of evil's facade, taunted me and pushed me down once he caught up with me at my doorstep, seeking to break my spirit and assert his dominion. But I'd jump back up, after which he pushed me down again, as he called me names. I didn't fight back, but neither did I stay down. He was relentless, and my younger sister happened to see me and by this time, witnessing the unfolding scene, trembled with fear, her heart heavy with worry for her sibling's safety.

In that pivotal moment, my father emerged from the shadows, a pillar of strength, who locked with me, and with a stern yet powerful voice, issued a demand. "Son, if you don't stand up to this bully, I'll make sure you regret it when you step inside this house." I knew my father meant what he said. We weren't very close but close enough that I knew he would stand by his words.

He was that sort of man. So now I was afraid of both Richard and my father. But I still stood there motionless, and Richard still didn't back down and proceeded to push my sister down as well. He felt invincible at this point. That just infuriated my father even worse. "Hit him back! Hit him back!" My sister was now sobbing, and I can still remember the smirk on the bully's face.

And so, a choice hung in the air, a decision that would change the course of my life. My father's words, a catalyst for transformation, echoed in my mind. Would I succumb to the bully, or would I rise to face my fears, defying the malevolence that sought to consume him? In a heartbeat, my resolve solidified like a diamond forged under immense pressure. My fists clenched, the adrenaline surged through my veins, and with newfound courage, I swung. Blow after blow, my spirit roared like a lion, my fists channeling the might of my will. Richard was shocked at the fist hitting him in the face, and then how I grabbed his neck and flipped him to the ground! I had no idea that I had it inside of me, but as the adrenaline started to flow, my arms and fists kept pummeling Richard Tory. Punch, punch, punch. I looked up at my father who was literally coaching me as I fought back. Looking back, I'm not so sure my father would not have ended up in jail today for coaxing his son to fight, but it was Jersey in the 1970s. The bully wrestled himself away from my grip and took off crying down the street. He never looked back, and he never bothered me again.

In that battle, both internal and external, I emerged victorious, a warrior who had discovered a strength within himself he never knew existed. The bully, shocked and humiliated, fled like a coward into the shadows, never to torment me again. And in the aftermath of that encounter, wisdom graced my ears, whispered in the tender embrace of his father's guidance. "Stand up for yourself, my son," his father imparted. "For in doing so, the victim within us ceases to exist."

I learned a powerful lesson that day, one that would shape the course of my life. It was not just about the physical confrontation, but about the courage to confront one's fears and rise against the darkness that seeks to oppress. In the streets of New Jersey, a hero was born that day, my name forever etched in the annals of our neighborhood. For in that moment, I discovered the truth: when we face our problems head-on, when we stand tall in the face of adversity, we awaken a powerful force within us—the force of resilience, strength, and the unwavering will to triumph over darkness.

What is my message to you? Remember the power that resides within you. In the face of your adversity, stand tall and fight back, for within you lies the strength to conquer what seeks to hold you back. As you walk the streets of life, maybe you'll be inspired by the hero who didn't let the bully steal his happiness. Allowing yourself to become a victim is no way to live, and the victim inside you ceases when you stand up in opposition to who and what is trying to push us down. Something powerfully intrinsic happens when you have the courage to confront your problems rather than cower to them. This is a powerful lesson I learned from my father on the streets of New Jersey in the 1970s, a man I never knew very well but who taught me this invaluable life lesson.

Standing Up for Myself

The neighborhood where I grew up was in East Newark, a predominantly working-class community, with a mix of residential, industrial, and commercial areas. Many residents worked in the nearby factories, which produced a range of goods, from textiles to chemicals. Most residents lived in row homes or small single-family homes. People worked very hard and were thick-skinned and tough as a result. But East Newark was also known for its tight-knit community, a strong sense of neighborhood spirit and a high level of civic engagement. We often gathered for social events, such as block parties and community festivals, and many families had lived in the town for generations, contributing to a sense of stability and continuity. It was a lot different than Portugal though, much more urban and densely populated.

We lived in a place where most of my neighbors were Polish or from Polish descent. There were also plenty of neighbors who were Italian. Back then, it wasn't uncommon to have Polish neighborhoods and Italian neighborhoods all mixed in with other families who didn't fit into their unwritten and unspoken rules. The cultural mix was confusing for me as a child because in Portugal, we were all Portuguese and we shared a common culture. I remember being confused and anxious.

I slowly and eventually acclimated to the culture, like most kids do, and my parents enrolled me in school where I was one of the few kids who didn't know English. I was darker skinned than most of the other kids as well, so I stood out like a sore thumb. It also seemed like a lifetime before I learned English. In the bustling classroom, where the laughter of children and the murmur of learning filled the air, there I sat, a young soul who felt like a solitary island adrift in a vast sea. As my peers chattered and bonded effortlessly, the words that surrounded me were all foreign. I might as well have been going to school on Mars! Even the teacher's voice, usually a source of guidance and knowledge, was distant and incomprehensible. Every instruction, every piece of knowledge, became a riddle that I struggled to decipher.

So, each new day became a journey into the unknown. Simple tasks felt like insurmountable challenges, and the fear of being misunderstood or left behind loomed like a shadow over my every move. No child should have to endure such an experience. It was a battle between two worlds—the world of the classroom, brimming with the promise of knowledge, and my longing to connect, to belong, and to make sense of this new reality. The desire to participate, to contribute, was palpable, yet it remained locked away like a caged bird.

Amidst my struggles, however, glimmers of resilience began to show through. In time, with the support and patience of my teachers and eventually, understanding peers, I learned the language and began to bridge the gap. I learned how to stand up for myself and, slowly but surely, the barriers started to crumble, and the once mysterious language began to unfold for me. Through perseverance and determination, the language of learning, communication, and connection. It was a journey of courage and growth, a testament to the resilience of the human spirit and particularly of immigrants and their children. In the end, it was a tale of triumph—a testament to the indomitable spirit of a young immigrant who faced the challenges of being the only child in a classroom who did not understand English and emerged stronger, wiser, and more connected. I never was a very good student, but not because I wasn't smart enough to be a good student, I just didn't care enough. Even so, I overcame the barriers set before me and assimilated into the culture.

Over the years, as I got older and told my friends of my experiences as a young immigrant, people would ask me if getting bullied and beat up led to anxiety and depression, or to other mental health issues as a child. I can honestly say, if it did, I really don't remember. I was a resilient child and although being an immigrant can also come with its own set of challenges, it was also an opportunity to start life in a new country. It taught me how to be independent and how to fend for myself. It became the cornerstone of how I lived the rest of my life, it was how I learned to stand up for myself.

Did you know that immigrants have a long history of entrepreneurship and starting successful businesses? A recent study found that immigrants were more likely to start businesses than members of the native population in most of the sixty-nine countries surveyed. In the United States, where 13.7 percent of the population is foreign-born, immigrants represent more than 20.2 percent of business owners. According to a 2018 study by the National Foundation for American Policy, immigrants have founded one-half of the United States' billion-dollar companies—so-called unicorns. So, while being a child immigrant was a tough thing to go through, I count myself blessed to have been one because it made me into a very resilient person.

I also believe that immigrants are less risk averse. Deciding to become an immigrant is a risky thing in and of itself. So once you've conquered that risk, other risks seem less scary. Many people look at risk and think, "What are the odds that I will succeed?" But I think about it differently. I ask myself instead, "What's the worst thing that would happen if I failed?"

It certainly can't be more difficult than anything I faced as a child on the streets of New Jersey! This is my mindset and it's partly what's made me a successful entrepreneur.

So, if you've been thinking about your own BIG idea, your dreams and aspirations, stop measuring the risk of trying. Instead measure the risk of not trying. Consider the worst thing that could happen if you never give it a chance. What are the odds you'll succeed if you never even try? Zero! Sure maybe you don't understand the language of the entrepreneur, but I promise once you stand up for yourself and your dreams, you'll be surprised at how much you can accomplish.

Kicking My Way to the Top

I could tell you many other stories about my childhood. Some would make you cry and others would make you laugh. Many I would like to forget, but they are what made me who I am today.

You are probably the same way. We can't avoid being molded by our past. But the important thing is to either try to let go of the bad things that happened, or try to allow them to teach you lessons you can use today. I'm an entrepreneur and cybersecurity expert, not a philosopher or theologian, and I don't know why

God allows certain bad things to happen to us, but I do know that we have the power to make choices. We can choose to make our lives better, or worse. No matter what environment you grew up in, whether it was in a nice, loving home with a white picket fence, in a public housing project, or maybe you had no home at all, you still have the power to choose. You can choose to complain and be envious of other people around you, or you can say to yourself, "I'm going to try to make the best of the situation." You can always kick your way to the top, like I did.

One last story I will share about my childhood is how my mother taught me to kick my way to the top. Early on when I arrived in America, when I was being bullied, I recall asking my mother if I could take karate lessons. If my memory serves me correctly, I must have been watching the 1970s martial arts TV programs and thought to myself, "If I only knew karate, then I wouldn't come home with the occasional black eye or bloody nose." Much to my surprise, my mother did enroll me in karate lessons, which I enjoyed and learned a lot from. It gave me a much needed boost of self-confidence.

In the mystical realm of karate, a journey of transformation unfolds, igniting this flame of confidence. Karate weaves a potent elixir, blending physical prowess, mental fortitude, and self-discovery. And as

I stepped onto the dojo's hallowed grounds, I began to see myself as a hero and not a victim. In this sacred space, I felt like I was entrusted with secrets that would help me survive. With each strike and block, I gained more and more confidence, and gradually the voices of doubt faded, replaced by an inner knowing that I possessed the strength to overcome my obstacles. With each belt earned, another seed of self-confidence took root, watered by the sweat of my hard work and dedication. I'm grateful that my mother allowed me this opportunity.

Why am I telling you this story?

In a famous sequence from *The Karate Kid*, teenager Daniel LaRusso asks Mr. Miyagi to teach him karate. Much to Daniel's surprise, his first "lesson" was to wax his teacher's car. He was to apply the wax on in one direction and then wipe it off in the other. Daniel did this day in and day out, thinking it was all a waste of his time, until he became frustrated and complained. But he soon learned that all those hours he spent waxing developed his muscle memory for defensive blocks. Similarly, karate also taught me how to develop my own "muscle memory." By that I don't necessarily mean physically, although that too, but also mentally and emotionally. It taught me not to be afraid. Even today it serves as a reminder that I can kick my way in and out of any situation. Today as

I lead a cybersecurity company; I still use my muscle memory. If I need to kick a door down to reach my goals, I've got some experience!

My message to you is that if you need to develop your own muscle memory, be bold and find ways to make that happen. It might not be karate, and of course there are many ways to pursue personal and professional development. Read books, attend seminars and conferences, and find a good church or a coach who can help you better define who you are and who you want to become. I know too many people who complain about their present situation but who refuse to find ways to self-improve. But once you begin the path to self-discovery, I promise you'll be surprised at how much inner-strength you possess. You too can kick your way to the top!

"No matter the voices that
whisper doubt, remember this:
your dreams are yours alone,
and no one has the power
to extinguish them."

2

Growing Up a Dreamer

Every child, it seems, is burdened with the weight of this message: study hard, do your homework, and get A's on your tests. It echoes in the corridors of academia, it's whispered by teachers, chanted by parents and by other well-meaning relatives, and sometimes even by friends. It's a proclamation that resonates through the ages of schooling, urging young minds to strive for excellence and to achieve those coveted good grades. But as with any melody, its reception varies from ear to ear.

For some children, they march forth with determination, setting their sights on academic glory. They are the aspirants, fueled by ambition and driven to excel. And lo and behold, they succeed, their report cards adorned with accolades, their dreams aligning with their achievements. But alas, the grand symphony encounters a few discordant notes. There are many children, like me, the innocent souls with dreams of their own, who find themselves out of tune with the

conventional path of academic excellence. Yes, my
aspirations were elsewhere, beyond the confines of the
classroom. I was not bound by a lack of intelligence
or potential; instead, I simply danced to the beat of
different drums. I was never the "study hard and get
good grades" type. My grades were not abysmal, but
they didn't excite teachers or my parents much either.
It was a mix of lack of engagement and of course the
added challenge of adjusting to a new language after
moving to America.

I was not lazy and certainly unintelligent. I was
simply like countless other boys who held dreams and
aspirations, but the traditional rigors of the classroom
held little allure. I remember when the day of graduation arrived, I breathed a sigh of relief, rejoicing that
school was over. The future beckoned, full of uncertainties and possibilities, and I pondered my next move.

By this time we had moved from New Jersey to
Florida, the West Palm Beach area. I was working
in local restaurants and starting to earn some serious
money, at least by "back then" standards. Despite my
average grades, I had a strong work ethic and I built fast
rapport with people. I loved working in the restaurant
business and I found myself making enough money to
buy things many of my friends couldn't afford. In fact,
I was quite proud that I was doing better than many
kids who outscored me in school with better grades. It

turns out that "real life" was a lot different than school, and I loved it. I worked as many shifts as I possibly could. It was not unusual for me to sometimes work a double shift, and once in a blue moon, I would even do a triple shift! What I lacked in academics, I made up for in hard work.

As the days rolled by and my determination held firm, I found myself amassing a considerable sum of money. It was a pot of gold, a treasure chest of dreams waiting to be unlocked. And so, one day, I made a decision that would forever alter the course of my life—I resolved to embark on a journey back to my homeland, a land that held the key to the enigma of my origins. The thought of venturing back to my roots ignited a spark of excitement within me as I envisioned stepping foot on the soil that cradled my earliest memories.

Beyond the prospect of reconnecting with my homeland, I also anticipated the thrill of meeting relatives I had only heard whispers of, or worse, had never heard of at all. I wondered if my mother would be receptive to my quest. I fretted over her reaction, fearing her disapproval or reluctance to delve into the past. But my worries proved unfounded, for she embraced my desire to revisit my home with open arms. Her joy mirrored mine, and she helped me prepare. I was proud of my mother who had become a chef for one of the most successful and wealthiest men in America. She and I shared not only a strong work ethic, but we were favored by both God and man.

And so, the days leading up to my departure were a whirlwind of emotions. The prospect of returning to my homeland stirred a cocktail of exhilaration and trepidation within me. What would await me there? Would the people open their arms to welcome me, or would they turn away, wary of the outsider who had returned? Memories, both joyous and sorrowful, danced in my mind. With every passing moment, the countdown to my journey drew closer, and I even wondered if my homeland might tempt me to stay forever. Or would it become a fleeting dream, leaving me yearning for the freedom of America once more?

My three-week odyssey began in France with a cousin I'd never met. Our shared adventures began with the rhythmic chugging of a train, transporting us to the City of Lights, Paris, where we explored, dined, and, of course, enjoyed fine wine. But our wanderlust did not cease at the borders of France; instead, it brought me to Portugal, a land that held a glimmer of forgotten reminiscences. The memories of my early years there had long been shrouded in time but the nostalgia that enveloped me was awakened. As I reconnected with long-lost relatives and friends, the threads of our shared bloodline woven intricately through time, I found myself not only gaining insight into my family's history but also unlocking windows to understanding my own self. I discovered nuances of my identity that had remained hidden. It was fun to see other people who looked and acted like me!

The journey of self-discovery continued as a dear friend loaned me a car, a 1968 Citroen Dyane 6. One of the notable features of this French car was its convertible top option. The fabric roof could be rolled back to create a quasi-convertible experience, allowing my friends and I to enjoy open-air driving as we navigated the foreign roads in our Citroen. As we cruised through the scenic landscapes of Portugal, up and down the coastline, the gentle purring of the engine provided a soothing soundtrack to my thoughts. It was an amazing adventure and I marveled at the intricate web of events that had led me on this transcontinental adventure.

A Drive to the Beach

Our spirits soared as we cruised the sun-kissed roads of Portugal in our trusty Citroen. We felt invincible, embracing the freedom of our youthful years. Oh, what a magical time it was! Southern Portugal, a haven of sun-soaked delight, welcomed us with open arms. Its allure was irresistible—an idyllic European holiday where the sun never ceased to shine, where ivory beaches caressed the azure waves, and where warm-hearted souls extended a hand of friendship. The charm of this enchanting region lay not only in its Mediterranean climate but in the people of southern Portugal who embodied a simple way of life. Amidst lush vineyards, rolling landscapes, and the coast, they nurtured their land and savored the simple joys that life offered. "Viva a boa vida," they would say, embracing the good life with zest and gratitude.

As it would, serendipity eventually led us to a real estate acquaintance of my friend. What was meant to be a casual meeting turned into a captivating exploration of beachfront property. The vista that stretched before us was akin to a dreamscape—a paradise of pristine beauty, reminiscent of West Palm Beach, but without the exorbitant price tag. My BIG idea mind started to churn.

With a mixture of courage and curiosity, I inquired about the cost of this slice of paradise, and to my astonishment, the answer was a mere $11,000. My heart raced with excitement, and the vision of owning my own oceanfront retreat began to take shape. This was a chance to seize a golden opportunity, to be part of the burgeoning development, and my mind swirled with dreams of expansion and growth. At the tender age of seventeen, the prospect of acquiring such a treasure was both thrilling and daunting. I pledged my serious interest, promising to return to the United States to secure the funds for this life-altering investment. The handshake that sealed the deal marked a moment of hopeful determination. I was soon going to become a European real estate developer. Who knew how much beachfront property I could end up owning!

Later, back on American soil, reality settled in, and I toiled diligently at the restaurant, hopeful that my hard-earned tips would eventually accumulate into the necessary sum. Despite my best efforts, the reality of financial constraints cast a shadow over my dreams. The fantasy of owning an oceanfront paradise began to slip through my fingers, and a tinge of regret lingered in my heart. That $11,000 investment became an elusive dream, one that slipped away like a sailboat on the waters, and my vision of becoming a European real estate mogul, thriving amid the bustling tide of multimillion-dollar condos, remained a captivating "what if".

But life, with its twists and turns, had its own plans and purposes for me. While I may not have owned a piece of Portugal's coastline, I embarked on a journey that led me to unforeseen adventures that would shape my destiny in ways I could never have imagined. Though the road diverged, it led me to new BIG ideas, reminding me that life's treasures come in many forms, and sometimes, the road not taken leads us to the most extraordinary destinations of all.

Allow Yourself to Dream BIG Dreams

Why did I tell you this story? I want you to dream BIG dreams, and don't be afraid to go after them. I was just a young man when I dreamed of owning beachfront property. Was it even possible? Probably not. But it did not stop me from my BIG dreams. Even as a teenager I didn't fear taking risks. Mark Twain once wrote, "Twenty years from now you will be more disappointed by the things you didn't do than by the ones you did. So throw off the bowlines. Sail away from the safe harbor. Catch the trade winds in your sails. Explore. Dream. Discover." I've always embodied this, and I feel that my calling is to help other people do the same.

Did you know that dreams are more than thoughts. You feel a dream in your bones and in your heart. John Maxwell writes, "I believe that each of us has a dream placed in our heart. I'm not talking about wanting to win the lottery. That kind of idea comes from a desire to escape our present circumstances, not to pursue a heartfelt dream. I'm talking about a vision deep inside that speaks to the very soul. It's the thing we were born to do. It draws on our talents and gifts. It appeals to our highest ideals. It sparks our feelings of destiny. It is inseparably linked to our purpose in life. The dream starts us on the success journey." Indeed, one dream leads to another, and to another. When you dream, you never know where you might end up!

I want to see you unlock the vault of your imagination and let your dreams take flight. Embrace the audacity of dreaming BIG. No matter the voices that whisper doubt, no matter the skeptics who cast shadows upon your aspirations, remember this: your dreams are yours alone, and no one has the power to extinguish the flames of your vision. The naysayers may scoff and attempt to squash your dreams like a bug on the sidewalk, but do not falter, for their limitations are not yours to bear. Yes, there may be setbacks, and failure may knock on your door, but the true essence of dreaming lies not in the outcome, but in the journey.

It's never too late to dream either. I was young when I had my first BIG dream to buy beachfront property. Sure, it's easy to have dreams when you're young. As you get older, people tend to lose their motivation to dream big. Life has a way of beating you down and holding you back. But this is also one of the great things about having a dream. You can pursue your dream no matter where you are today. What happened in the past isn't as important as what lies ahead in the future. As the saying goes, "No matter what a person's past may have been, his future is spotless." Sure, you're not a kid anymore, and you might have forgotten how to dream. But the good news is, you can always remember how, if you want to. Dream big, my friend!

"The people we encounter along our journey are not random encounters; they are purposeful and placed in our lives for a reason."

3

Faith in the Impossible

In the bustling culinary world of West Palm Beach, Florida, I found myself immersed in a profession that offered more than just the art of serving delectable dinners. Working tirelessly in local restaurants, I embraced the opportunity to connect with a diverse array of people, including the city's elite—the rich and the famous. Building swift rapport with these influential personalities became an art form that I honed with passion and skill, and I became quite well-known for it as well.

Amidst the winter of 1984, a pivotal moment in my journey arrived when fate steered me toward an extraordinary encounter with Paul W. Pandorf II, a coworker of remarkable wisdom. Our rapid connection would prove to be no mere coincidence, but rather I believe destiny. I believe that every experience, every connection, has a purpose, and Paul was no exception. As I reflect upon our fortuitous friendship, I'm reminded of the power of meaningful relationships in shaping one's entrepreneurial path. A business venture is not merely a solitary journey, but a dynamic network of connections. That's why I'm a big believer in building relationships.

Now, Paul epitomized the spirit of personal growth and development, seeking growth in every moment, devouring books during the restaurant's downtimes. His eloquence and sharp intellect became a source of inspiration for me. The qualities I admired in him—artful articulation and profound thinking—became guideposts in my own journey to success. A wise leader seeks not only to impart knowledge but also to absorb wisdom from others, an unending exchange that empowers both mentor and mentee.

Paul had also once attended the Virginia Military Institute (VMI) and often spoke of its transformative impact. Despite not graduating from VMI, Paul possessed an unwavering belief in the power of military bearing and its potential to unlock greatness. One day, Paul shared his observation with me. "Carlos," he said, "You possess the military bearing—a rare quality that sets you apart. Have you ever considered exploring options beyond the restaurant business? Your potential knows no bounds."

Intrigued yet unsure, I hesitated, dismissing the idea of VMI as incongruent with my immediate future. The allure of business success seemed captivating enough, and I never considered anything like the military or even college. But Paul's observation stuck with me until I saw the cinematic masterpiece *Top Gun*, which ignited a spark within me—a yearning for speed, adventure, and self-discovery. Inspired, I began to reconsider the notion of attending a military institute and joining the ranks of the military. Soon VMI became an enticing possibility—an institution that promised to nurture my potential and shape my destiny beyond imagination.

I sought Paul's guidance in navigating the labyrinthine application process for VMI. Together, we meticulously filled out the application, crafting a letter that showcased my unique strengths and aspirations. Brimming with hope, I mailed the application just before the deadline, only to soon afterwards receive a disheartening rejection letter. The dream that once seemed within reach now felt unattainable, and the future seemed uncertain. But I don't easily let dreams die. This was merely a detour, a momentary pause, and with unyielding optimism, I started to work on my Plan B to attend VMI.

I Refuse to Take No for an Answer

In the scorching summer of 1985, I was still working in the restaurant business, but still thinking about my Plan B dream to attend VMI. The allure of Virginia Military Institute (VMI) called to me like a beacon, and I couldn't ignore the pull toward a new and exciting future. Armed with an audacious dream, I made the decision to take a trip to Lexington, Virginia, and to personally walk into the halls of VMI and enroll. It was an audacious idea, but one I felt certain would be successful. I then stumbled upon a unique opportunity with a company called Auto Drive Away. This company offered me a chance to transport a sleek Corvette from Florida to Charleston, South Carolina, which was closer to Lexington, Virginia, than I was sitting in West Palm Beach, Florida. So, determined to reach my final destination of VMI, I took the wheel of the bright orange stingray and raced through the open roads with the wind in my hair and dreams in my heart. I barrelled up I-95 knowing for certain I would soon be a VMI cadet. My arrival in Charleston marked only the beginning of the journey though, as the final road to VMI still lay ahead, and I needed to cover another 444 miles to reach Lexington, Virginia. Undeterred by the distance, I continued my trip as a hitchhiker until I reached VMI's hallowed halls.

As I stepped foot onto the hallowed grounds of VMI, an overwhelming sense of awe and wonder engulfed me. The campus stood before me like a majestic fortress of knowledge and discipline, unlike anything I had ever encountered. The imposing Gothic architecture, adorned with intricate details and noble spires, spoke of a heritage that embraced everything America stands for.

The well-manicured lawns and stately buildings exuded an aura of excellence. Every corner seemed to hold a piece of history, and the walls seemed to whisper tales of valor and triumph that echoed through history. As I walked through the post, I could also sense the determination of the cadets. Their sense of purpose and camaraderie was contagious, and I knew I was in the right place. Here, I would be molded and shaped into a leader, armed with knowledge and equipped with the values of honor, integrity, and resilience.

But a formidable challenge stood before me, gaining entry into the Admissions Office without a prior appointment. With sheer determination, I politely convinced the receptionist to grant me a brief meeting with Colonel Buchanan, the Director of Admissions who had sent me the rejection letter. It wasn't easy to get past the receptionist, but finally successful and armed with my rejection letter as a symbol of my unwavering spirit, I managed to secure a mere five minutes of the Colonel's time.

As I stepped into the Colonel's office, I remember feeling the weight of the moment. I was of course quite nervous, but also determined. It was a very impressive office, lots of mahogany, dark wood, and brass here and there, something you would expect to find in a military leader's office. For a split second, it reminded me of that Jack Nicholson movie, *A Few Good Men*, and I was about to find out if the Colonel could handle "my truth." So how was I going to convince this tall and foreboding Colonel to let me into VMI? I had no idea!

To convince the Colonel, I needed more than eloquent words; I needed to demonstrate to him my unwavering commitment to become a successful VMI cadet. I stood motionless and told him why I loved my country and why I would be a standout cadet. I explained how I drove seventeen hours to see him, and that I was hoping he could share with me what I needed to do to be accepted as a student. He looked intrigued, and replied, "Son, I really don't know anything about you, but let me pull out your file and figure this out." He asked me to sit and wait a little bit. My file, of course, was unimpressive and he impatiently declined my request for admission, but I wasn't giving up easily. I pressed him further and I think he finally recognized my internal fortitude. "Carlos," he told me, "if you go home and enroll in a local community college, and demonstrate to me that you can successfully compete in an academic environment, I promise you that I'll reevaluate your admission for VMI's class next year."

Carrying the Colonel's words as a beacon of hope, I found my way back to Florida and headlong into college. I worked tirelessly, transforming from a below average student into an exceptional scholar. I worked and studied, worked and studied. Remember I was not a good student as a younger man. But not because I wasn't intelligent. This time I had something to aim for, and I shot for the center of the target and ended the year with a 3.25 GPA. Not exceptional but a world of difference from the low 2s in high school. I even surprised myself! When the time came, I presented my grades to the Colonel, to his surprise. I surmise he never expected to see me again. But when I walked back into his office more than a year later, report card in hand, he honored his word and accepted my admission into VMI. He was proud, I could tell, and I was now determined to make him proud again.

My dream had finally taken root, and I soon soared to new heights as a VMI student. Excelling academically, I earned the admiration and recognition of both peers and faculty. The transformation was astounding——a once-average student had become a shining example of determination and tenacity. The work at VMI was challenging and the environment was highly disciplined. But my father had me well-trained. For better or for worse, my father was a tough disciplinarian, which prepared me for my time at VMI. My transition from civilian life to military life was not difficult as a result.

In fact, at my graduation, my father, whom I had not always seen eye to eye with, shed a tear of pride. This was the first and only time I saw my father cry. My journey of relentless determination had not only earned the admiration of others but also my father. He was a man of few words but the tears told a story I will never forget.

Today, I still carry with me a quote I once had the opportunity to share with Colonel Buchanan as a reminder of my triumph over adversity. In a letter to the Colonel, I quoted Benjamin Disraeli: "The secret to success in life is for a man to be ready for his opportunity when it comes." I like to think that this story serves as an inspiring testament to the power of unwavering resolve, the resilience to overcome rejection, and the relentless pursuit of dreams. From the rejection of a single letter to the transformation of a lifetime, my journey is a tale of inspiration and empowerment. A life changed, my destiny redefined,

I went from restaurant worker to VMI graduate and service in the United States Air Force.

Lessons in Determination

When I look back at my decision to drive from West Palm Beach, Florida, to Lexington, Virginia, with only a rejection letter in hand, I ask myself: what lessons did I learn? It's an important thing to look back and learn from your past. I can point to three lessons, and I hope you can also learn the same from my story.

First, dreams are like seeds planted within us, waiting for the nurturing touch of belief and determination to bring them to fruition. My journey to VMI began with a small seed of possibility, an idea that I wasn't initially too enthused about. But like all seeds, it yearned to grow, and I refused to let it wither away. Our dreams are the beacons that guide us through life, illuminating the path toward our God-given purpose. And yet, it's easy to ignore these quiet whispers in our hearts, dismissing them as mere fantasies. But here's the truth: dreams have an inherent power, an inexhaustible energy that demands attention and action. If you dare to embrace them, they will reward you with greatness beyond imagination.

Second, simply acknowledging our dreams is not enough; we must take action. As I share the story of my journey to VMI, I am met with chuckles and even laughter. Driving to a prestigious institution without an appointment, uncertain of what awaits, may seem crazy to many. Yet, the pursuit of audacious dreams often demands bold and unconventional actions. When your dreams are colossal, you must be willing to take extraordinary measures to achieve them. Embrace the madness of your aspirations! The world may call it crazy, but it is the audacity of the dreamers that has propelled humanity forward throughout history. Let your passion lead you, and don't shy away from doing whatever it takes to bring your dreams to life. Be persistent, for true success belongs to those who refuse to relent.

Third, in the pursuit of our dreams, the power of relationships cannot be underestimated. The people we encounter along our journey are not random encounters; they are purposeful connections placed in our lives for a reason. My friend's influence nudged me in the direction of VMI, forever altering the course of my life. Recognize the value of those who inspire and support you. Cherish your relationships, for they are the keys to unlocking doors of opportunity you never knew existed.

I urge you to cultivate the seeds of your dreams and pursue them with all your heart. Embrace the audacious, take bold action, and cherish the relationships that propel you forward. Trust in the power of faith to guide you through the most challenging moments. As you do, you will discover that dreams are not merely figments of imagination; they are the architects of a life that defies limits and knows no boundaries. The world is waiting for your dreams to unfold, and when you embrace them with unwavering belief, nothing can stand in your way. Have faith and let the extraordinary adventure of your dreams begin. Only faith is able to grasp the reality of the possible in the face of the impossible. Only faith has the power to move seemingly impossible mountains. Have faith, my friend!

"If you're still waiting on
your purpose on this earth,
your life mission, don't stand
still and wait. Do anything
but stand still."

4

Finding Purpose in a Limousine

In my late twenties, after my experience at VMI and in the Air Force, I was unsure of my next move. The education I received was unparalleled and the skills I learned as an airman were invaluable, but I was still searching for God's purpose for my life. I happen to believe each of us has a mission in life, and that we aren't truly living our best life until we discover what that is, and dedicate our lives to pursuing it. At this time in my life, I still hadn't discovered my mission, but I was also not willing to put my life on pause, get lazy, or waste away what I had learned. I was also recently married and expecting a child, so I kept moving despite not knowing my direction.

I love the quote about times in your life when you have to wait. "Things may come to those who wait, but only the things left by those who hustle." That's exactly what I did, I kept hustling, and in an effort to advance myself and support my new family, and to repair my broken relationship with my father, I went into the limousine business. The limousine business?

My father was a limousine driver and I surmised if I did the same, our relationship might improve. Frankly, I can say that it did not make much of a difference, but the experience proved to be life-changing. Before I explain why and how, I want to encourage you to keep hustling.

Don't let any time go to waste. During periods of waiting, time is all you have. So put it to good use. The longer you're lazy, the longer it will take to find your calling in life.

So again, I bought a limousine franchise, which simply means that I got a shiny new limousine and a small customer list to get launched. A successful limo business is built on referrals, so I treated my customers like royalty as I drove them around Florida's treasure coast and down to south Florida. It didn't matter who got into my car, they were my VIPs and I catered to their every need, making sure they were comfortable and arrived safely to their destination. Fortunately word spread, and this is when things suddenly and unexpectedly changed for me. God knew exactly what He was doing with me when I bought my limousine.

In the 1990s, and even today, West Palm Beach where I lived and mostly drove from, was a magnet for the rich, successful, and famous. So, as I drove them around, I decided I was going to learn from them. My limousine became my own personal success laboratory. One by one, entrepreneurs, CEOs, business leaders, political leaders, famed musicians and athletes would get into my luxury automobile. I was careful not to pry or bother, but I also found that my customers almost always gladly offered their advice and they liked to tell stories from their own lives. The stature of my customers began to grow as word must have gotten out that I was the best limousine driver on Florida's southeast coast.

On a sun-drenched day in Florida, one chance encounter changed the course of my life. It was a day like any other, but little did I know that a man of great influence and wisdom would step into my car and leave an indelible mark on my soul. The man who graced my car with his presence was none other than Robert Schuller, a renowned California clergyman whose ministry had grown from preaching in a humble drive-in movie theater to a vast empire of inspiration. His reach extended far beyond the confines of any pulpit; he was a best-selling author, an enthralling speaker, and the charismatic host of the widely acclaimed "Hour of Power" television show, which drew millions of devoted viewers from all corners of the globe. The power of his message transcended borders and touched hearts around the world.

As destiny would have it, I found myself in the unique position of driving this esteemed man of faith and vision, and our time together became an extraordinary opportunity to absorb his boundless wisdom and motivation. With each moment that passed, I felt incredibly fortunate to be in his presence.

One day, in a moment of playful spontaneity, Schuller shared a daring idea with me. He asked me to drive the limousine I was chauffeuring onto the airport runway to surprise his wife, who was arriving from California. My instincts hesitated, as I knew well the strict regulations surrounding airport operations. However, Schuller's spirit of resilience and fearlessness prevailed, and with a few calls to the airport, the plan was set in motion.

In retrospect, I realized that Schuller's philosophy was at play during that exhilarating escapade. "Never bring the problem-solving stage into the decision-making stage," he once wrote. In essence, he taught me the art of focusing on solutions rather than being overwhelmed by problems. His insistence on driving down the runway to greet his wife symbolized his profound belief in seizing the moment and embracing the possibilities that life presented, even in the face of seemingly insurmountable obstacles.

As I steered the limousine down the runway, I felt an overwhelming rush of emotions. The thrill of the moment was coupled with the realization that life is about more than adhering to conventions; it is about daring to dream, taking bold actions, and embracing life's adventures with an unwavering spirit. Schuller's influence extended far beyond those fleeting moments. He had instilled in me a newfound appreciation for the power of faith, the importance of seizing opportunities, and the significance of cherishing every relationship that crosses our path. The memories of driving Schuller toward that awaiting airplane still fill my heart with gratitude and awe.

When I didn't have a customer in my limousine, I'd listen to motivational cassette tapes, which were very popular at the time. One of my favorite motivational speakers was a man named Brian Tracy. Brian Tracy was a motivational speaker and self-development author. He is the author of over eighty books that have been translated into dozens of languages. His popular books include *Earn What You're Really Worth*, *Eat That Frog!*, and *No Excuses!* I always loved what Tracy wrote about dreams and big ideas, "All successful people are big dreamers. They imagine what their future could be, ideal in every respect, and then they work every day toward their distant vision, that goal or purpose."

So the day Brian Tracy stepped into my limousine was a moment that caught me completely off guard yet filled me with an exhilarating mix of shock and elation. Having known him from his public persona as a dynamic sales trainer, speaker, and author, I was captivated by the opportunity to drive such an esteemed man around the vibrant landscape of south Florida. Little did I know that this encounter would reveal a side of Brian Tracy I didn't expect. I quickly realized that the man before me was different from the exuberant persona I had witnessed on stage. Brian Tracy was introspective and quiet, seemingly embodying the traits of an introvert, a surprising contrast to his confident and charismatic public image. It was a valuable reminder that some of the most powerful personalities may find their true essence in solitude, away from the spotlight.

Despite his reserved demeanor, I couldn't help but be impressed by the intensity in his gaze and the unwavering focus he maintained. It was evident that he was a man on a mission, a man who knew exactly what he wanted to achieve and was resolute in his pursuit of success. His professionalism was unmatched, and I admired the way he carried himself with unwavering determination.

I made sure to respect his privacy, avoiding intrusive questions or attempts to pry into his personal life. I knew that some level of distance was essential to ensure the comfort of my esteemed clients. Yet, every now and then, I couldn't help but steal glances at the enigmatic man in the rearview mirror, inspired by the aura of greatness that surrounded him. Brian Tracy's presence left another indelible mark on me. Witnessing his poise and composure, I found myself yearning to emulate the same sense of unshakable confidence and success. The way he carried himself was a testament to the power of self-assurance and the ability to remain focused amidst the chaos of life.

If they ever awarded MBA degrees from the luxurious confines of a limousine, I would have proudly claimed the title of being the first recipient. My journey as a limousine driver also brought me face to face with some of the most influential and accomplished individuals, including the legendary Jack Welch, a name synonymous with business excellence and visionary leadership. John Francis Welch, Jr., or Jack Welch as the world knew him, was an American business magnate, chemical engineer, prolific writer, and the renowned Chairman and CEO of General Electric. His rise to the pinnacle of corporate success made him an iconic figure and one of the most admired CEOs in history. However, to me, he was not just a larger-than-life figure, he was also my valued customer.

Every time Jack Welch stepped into my limousine, a sense of awe washed over me. He brought with him an aura of wisdom and an unwavering determination to impart knowledge and mentor those around him. As we drove together, he would sit beside me in the front row, while his management team occupied the back seats. It was an incredible privilege to have a front-row seat to his guidance and teachings, a position I cherished deeply.

One of the most significant lessons I learned from Welch was his approach to leadership and talent management. He once wrote, "If you pick the right people and give them the opportunity to spread their wings and put compensation as a carrier behind it, you almost don't have to manage them." Through his actions and words, he exemplified the art of identifying exceptional individuals and empowering them to shine in their respective roles.

Welch's philosophy of nurturing talent left an indelible mark on me. When I later ascended to the position of CEO myself, I embraced his principles and made it my mission to seek out and develop the right people for my team. Inspired by Welch's leadership philosophy, I took the time to recognize the potential in others and provided them with the platform to grow and thrive.

As time passed, I found myself deeply influenced by Jack Welch's mentorship, and his wise counsel bore fruit in my professional journey. Many years later, I established the ACS Cyber SEAL Program, a visionary initiative designed to attract the brightest minds in the cybersecurity domain. This program was a testament to Welch's enduring influence, as it mirrored his belief in empowering individuals and nurturing their talents.

John Henry may not be a name that immediately rings a bell for everyone, but his story is one of remarkable success and ingenuity. Unlike many others, John chose a different path, forgoing a college degree to delve into the intricate world of trading corn and soybean futures. It was through this unconventional journey that he honed his skills in hedging the price risk of holding these commodities, eventually developing cutting-edge mathematical and mechanical trend following methods for managing future trading accounts. His innovative concepts quickly gained traction, captivating brokerage firms across America and propelling him toward becoming a multi-billionaire and a prominent entrepreneur, including ownership of the Boston Red Sox and *The Boston Globe*.

It was during another fortuitous encounter that I had the privilege of meeting John Henry, although it was some time after he had achieved his immense success. As I chauffeured him around south Florida, I couldn't help but notice the laser-like focus he dedicated to his work. He epitomized the art of being present-minded, immersing himself fully in his business affairs while entrusting his assistant to take care of other aspects of his life. A key lesson I learned from John was the art of effective management. He described himself as a tough manager, constantly questioning assumptions and seeking pragmatic solutions. The wisdom he shared with me resonated deeply, instilling in me a curiosity-driven approach to leadership. To this day, I maintain a habit of unendingly asking questions and never ceasing to learn from my experiences and those around me.

John Henry's penchant for salesmanship was also evident in the way he impressed guests by arranging helicopter flights along the picturesque beaches of Florida. He understood the power of leaving a lasting impression and knew the value of showcasing his ventures in the most memorable ways. My encounter with John Henry not only offered a glimpse into the mind of a visionary entrepreneur but also left a lasting impact on my own leadership philosophy. His willingness to question, learn, and empower those around him became my guiding mantra, and his influence continues to shape my professional journey.

Robert Schuller, Brian Tracy, Jack Welch, Jr., and John Henry. There were many more as well, my customers who also became my mentors. To some people, driving a limousine might have appeared to be a step down for this VMI graduate and veteran of America's armed forces. Some of my former classmates and comrades-in-arms were achieving great things and defending our country with honor. Me? I was still undecided about what to do with my life. But I hustled and got behind the steering wheel. All I did was drive a car, but what a drive it turned out to be. I learned from the greatest. I learned how to start a business, how to run a business, how to grow a business, and how to be the kind of leader I always wanted to be. My days as a limousine driver were not a wilderness experience because I made it more than that. I used the time to be a sponge, to amass information and to network with people who made a difference in my life. I eventually sold my car when a friend invited me to the Washington, D.C. Metro Area, to join a large government contractor, delivering what would later become known as Cybersecurity services and solutions. This is when and where my mission was born. But if not for my limousine, I'd never have learned what I would someday need to become an entrepreneur and CEO.

If you're still waiting on your purpose on this earth, your life mission, I encourage you to get behind the wheel and start to drive. Not literally, but figuratively. Don't stand still and wait. Walk and wait. Run and wait. Do anything but stand still. You never know when, where, and how you're going to receive the education you need to achieve your purpose. For me, I learned what I needed in a luxury automobile. I doubt that will be you, but I guarantee if you're patient enough and willing to work hard while you learn, you will eventually find your BIG idea. My mentor, Brian Tracy, once said, "Your greatest asset is your earning ability. Your greatest resource is your time." So start using your time to your advantage. If that's all you've got, then I'd say you're pretty lucky. Get to hustling today!

"Life is all about relationships.

At the end of the day,

that's really all you have

is your relationships.

Keep them strong."

5

The Entrepreneurial Way

I wasn't born an entrepreneur. Nobody is born an entrepreneur. I believe some people are born with an entrepreneurial spirit, which might mean they are more prone to take calculated risks in life, but I've learned that every entrepreneur is different and that it's not something that just comes to you automatically. There isn't a single personality trait or characteristic that makes one a good entrepreneur, so when I'm asked, I don't have a simple answer for people. But I do know how I personally learned how to start and grow a business, and how I discovered and refined my ability to seed BIG ideas. It didn't just magically happen. It took coaching, mentoring, and a lot of trial and error. In this chapter, I'll share what I've learned and how I put it to good use. I hope you can learn from my story and join me in my entrepreneurial journey.

After I left the Air Force and became more engaged with Amway as an independent business owner. I remember feeling so enthusiastic about becoming a business owner, I could hardly wait to get out of bed in the morning. Early on in one's entrepreneurial journey, the feelings are almost all positive. How could they not be? To be the master of one's destiny is an exciting thing indeed. Later, I learned that even if your business is successful, entrepreneurship comes with a mix of inspiring days and challenging days. Life as a business owner will be riddled with challenges, obstacles and hurdles that you'll need to overcome in order to achieve the success you desire. I think it's vitally important, however, to remember the early days of your business when it was all fun. That's when your entrepreneurial mental and emotional foundation was created. It's the honeymoon part of the journey. And just like in a marriage, it is important to look back and remember what brought you and your business together in the first place. It will help keep you going when the going gets tough.

My independent Amway business began to grow, and soon they asked me to travel internationally to speak with other independent owners. It was an exciting time because as I increased in my success, I was recognized for it and I was able to help others start and grow their businesses as well. Even today I enjoy talking to and coaching other people who want to become entrepreneurs. I love the relationships I've built over the years.

Zig Ziglar once wrote, "You don't build a business, you build people, then people build the business." Indeed, the first thing I learned is to value my relationships. When you're direct selling, you are selling yourself as much or more than you are selling your product. So I learned how to build fast rapport with people, which is really nothing more than spending quality time with them, listening and responding with optimism, and to be encouraging. You'll be surprised how fast you'll make new friends if you simply take time to be their friend. Then you'll have a friend for life. I've actually been accused of staying in relationships for too long. But I believe life is all about relationships. At the end of the day, that's really all you have is your relationships. So I say keep them and keep them strong. Don't burn bridges, if at all possible. If there is mutual trust and respect, stay the course. If there is not, you might still stay the course and be patient with it. Sometimes success comes much later than expected in life, and that includes your relationships.

Second, I learned effective sales strategies, including how to identify customer needs, address objections, and close sales. Closing sales is, for most people, a complex and intimidating task. But Amway showed me how to close sales with ease. You might think that selling soap can't help teach you how to sell more expensive and complex products, but you're wrong! Many of the closing strategies I learned decades ago with Amway, I still use today when I sell our Cybersecurity products and services, which are of course very complicated and expensive. To me it makes no difference what you're selling. The same sales strategies work no matter what you're selling, and unless you're an effective closer you won't ever become a great salesperson. While there are many salespeople who are savvy at opening a sale opportunity, but few who are effective closers. I learned how to be both.

The best closers don't get lost throwing information, technical jargon, and figures at their prospects—hoping most of it sticks enough to land a deal. That approach is far too one-sided. Instead, great closers work with prospects to ensure that a sale is mutually beneficial. For instance, when the time comes to talk about pricing and implementation, exceptional closers tend to already have the context they need to make a compelling recommendation.

That comes from working closely with their prospects and maintaining an active back-and-forth so that there are no surprises that may derail the sale. Surprises and sales tend not to mix well—in that context, they're often a result of insufficient due diligence. The best closers make it a priority to understand everything a prospect is evaluating as early on as possible, so they can provide value in these areas throughout the sales process. They never reach what they believe to be the end of a sales process, only to suddenly learn that the buyer has major concerns they never considered or addressed earlier on.

I also learned to create genuine urgency when I close a sale. Salespeople who reliably close never rely on the promise of a discount or sale to get the deal over the finish line. Pricing should never be the main reason to buy right now—as opposed to next week, month, or year. Great closers find a legitimate, pressing issue or opportunity related to their offerings. They start by helping a prospect understand that it's in their best interest to purchase as soon as possible. They know they can work with that buyer to figure out the exact terms after—and if they do it right, those terms won't include a sale or a discount. When we sell cybersecurity products and services, we of course never depend on sales and discounts. We strive to offer the most secure services and solutions by the best experts in the industry, so I'm glad I learned early on not to depend on slashing prices to get a sale. You shouldn't either.

Beyond closing sales, Amyway also taught me how to make effective and winning presentations. If you aren't able to stand up in front of a group and persuade them, you'll always struggle as a leader and entrepreneur. Leadership is about persuasion, and oftentimes that means standing in front of others and presenting your ideas. I learned how to clearly define the purpose and objective of my presentations, understand my audience's needs, interests, and knowledge level so I could customize my delivery style. I also learned how a strong opening and closing are vital to captivate my audience, as well as using simple, easy-to-digest language when I spoke. While eloquence is always impressive, an audience appreciates direct and easy-to-understand communication as well. I also learned how to incorporate interesting stories, which of course I have many! As an entrepreneur, there will be many occasions where you'll be called to present in front of at least a few people and probably many. You'll present to bankers, investors, employees, vendors, customers, and probably many other groups. So it's essential that you understand what it means to give a good presentation, and practice enough to feel comfortable with giving them. It will give you an edge over your competition!

Lastly, but probably most importantly, I learned how to identify opportunities. When operating an independent Amway business, I discovered how important it was to be on the constant lookout for others who might also want to become business owners. My independent business would grow exponentially as I discovered others who wanted to work with me, so my success was contingent upon their success. As a result,

I became very good at finding the "right" people, in other words the right opportunity. Not everyone is a good fit to be an independent business owner. But over time I learned who might be and who probably might not be. This is something I continued to think about for the rest of my career, up to today.

Although many aspiring entrepreneurs identify an idea for a new business, the question remains. Is the idea a viable business opportunity? In other words, does it fulfill a market need, solve a customer pain point, or improve an existing product? Perhaps you want to assess whether your business idea is viable, or you like the concept of entrepreneurship and are searching for the right opportunity to jump in. Either way, you need to familiarize yourself with different types of business opportunities and learn to identify them. Sometimes it takes a disruptive mindset, but not always. Sometimes the best ideas are simple and sitting right there in front of your eyes. I identified cybersecurity as an opportunity before many others did. I was certainly not the first, but I could foresee how "hackers" would soon wreak havoc on our government and on private business. In other words, I saw a market need. Later in this book, I'll share specifically how I addressed that need, but for now I'll share very simply that I was able to "see" the future and apply what I could see in the form of a business.

This brings me to one of the most frequently asked questions I'm asked by others who want to become entrepreneurs. How can I identify business opportunities? With a foundational understanding of the types of opportunities that exist, you can dive into identifying them. Here are three ways you can do so and examples to learn from.

Identify Pain Points

When searching for potential market needs, start with yourself. In your everyday life, what processes or tasks bother you? What's the job to be done that you haven't quite found the perfect product to fulfill? Many successful entrepreneurial ventures began with a personal problem in the founder's life. I cannot say that cybersecurity was a personal pain point for me, but I could definitely see how it was becoming a pain point for the government and for business. Also, a pain point others weren't serving well, so there was a gap in the market.

Conduct Market Research

I did not literally conduct my own market research, but I was surrounded by others in the industry so I was able to see and understand things much like a market researcher. But you may want to because another way to prove whether a business idea is viable is by conducting your own research. This includes using industry research to define the competitive landscape and determine your target audience, as well as interviewing or surveying people who fit your target demographics. Observing and gathering feedback from real people enables you to consider their perspectives and gain a deeper understanding of their motivations, frustrations, fears, and desires. This can help you conceptualize whether your product addresses a job to be done and the size of the audience that could benefit from it.

Question Processes

You can also identify business opportunities by examining the processes and delivery methods of existing product or service offerings. Try to evaluate each process with an open mind and ask questions about how you could improve it, such as:

- Could this process be faster?

- Could this process be executed using a more cost effective business model?

- Is there a more sustainable way to execute this process?

- Does this process exclude certain groups of people? If so, is there a way to make the process accessible to all?

You don't have to reinvent the wheel to break into entrepreneurship—you just need to recognize the potential for innovation that already exists.

I'm sure there are many other ways to identify a winning business opportunity. There are no rules, and for me, I simply do what I learned decades ago. I constantly scan the horizon looking for people and ideas that might be disruptive. When searching for business and market opportunities, always try to lead with a disruptive lens. Try to identify customer needs that aren't being fulfilled, or maybe fulfilled but with gaps. Rather than directly challenge companies dominating market segments, sometimes you can identify people who are over or underserved by existing offerings and compete on a disruptive level.

In the next chapter I'll share more about building a company through the growth stage. Starting a company is indeed a challenge, but growing a company is a much bigger challenge.

"It's easy to fall into half-heartedness. By that I mean you don't take a stand for anything. You ride the fence. That's no way to live."

6

Finding Faith in My Dreams

S o far I've not made any mention of the most important thing in my life: my relationship with God. That's because I didn't meet Jesus until I was in the Air Force. Up until then, I lived my life by my rules and I worshiped nobody but myself. If you don't have a relationship with God, if you're not a Christian, I hope you don't put this book down. I have the utmost respect for you and whatever you believe. You might not believe in God at all, or you might believe in God but in a different way than I do. My intent is not to argue or to antagonize. In fact, the Bible commands me, "If it is possible, as far as it depends on you, live at peace with everyone" (Romans 12:18). That being said, I want to tell you how Jesus changed the trajectory of my life. So, I hope you will have an open mind and heart as you read these words.

As you might imagine, the life of an airman can be filled with some intense and busy days, but then also some mundane and boring days. This see-saw effect has an impact on one's mental health and as a result many airmen resort to drugs and alcohol. Alcohol is readily available on and near military bases and is frequently used as a way to socialize and bond. I learned this soon after leaving VMI and joining the Air Force, 315th Training Squadron. The culture was steeped in it, and of course I gladly participated. When on-duty, I was focused on my service and I did a good job. But when off-duty, I partied with the best of them. I served the United States of America and myself, and nobody else. I was in the center of my universe and on the outside I was happy and enjoying life.

But there was something tugging at me. I couldn't identify the root problem at the time, but I often had feelings of shallowness and emptiness. I knew there must be more to life than parties. I was smart, determined, focused, and I did strive to be a man of integrity. So, I had an internal struggle inside of me, I would say it was a struggle for my soul, although I didn't really know or understand it at the time. I was a good airman, yes, but in many ways I was not a good person. And although I might have appeared to be happy, the truth was that I wasn't. I also felt there was a lack of purpose and destiny in my life. Who was I, really? Where was I headed? Why did I do the things I did?

Feelings of unfulfillment and loneliness plague the human race. We all have feelings of emptiness, which spills over into all areas of life, and often leads to depression and anxiety. It's a terrible feeling to wake up in the morning and go to bed at night feeling like your life is pointless and useless. To have no purpose and no higher meaning is something most of us cannot endure for a lifetime. Faith is the substance of things not seen, and if you can't see your purpose, then you've got no hope. This sums up how I was feeling about life at the time. My sinful actions weren't helping me feel better about my life. They made me feel worse.

Then I met a new friend. He piqued my curiosity because he seemed more joyful and content than most people I've met throughout my life. I was invited by my friend to a business meeting hosted by a company called Amway. He told me that Amway was looking for entrepreneurs who wanted to learn how to earn more income. I was of course always interested in making more money, as my military compensation wasn't very good. So, I told my friend I'd be happy to attend, and I was looking forward to learning more about entrepreneurship, my favorite topic!

Amway, a name that resonates widely, has garnered both praise and criticism over the years. Established in 1959 by the visionary minds of Jay Van Andel and Richard DeVos, this American direct sales company has flourished into an industry giant, reporting astounding sales nearing the $10 billion mark. Amway's product offerings span health, beauty, home care, and nutrition, captivating millions of individuals seeking to carve their own path to financial prosperity. You might have come across various perspectives about Amway, but contrary to the misinterpretations that surround some multi-level marketing companies, Amway operates distinctively. It is not a "pyramid scheme," nor does it rely on the recruitment of new members to generate income for existing business owners. Instead, the foundation of Amway's success lies in the sale of quality products to end consumers. The Amway business model epitomizes the spirit of entrepreneurship, empowering individuals to seize control of their financial destinies. Countless people have found solace in the opportunity to supplement their income while charting their unique course to success. By choosing Amway, they embark on a journey of financial independence, fueling their ambitions through hard work, dedication, and strategic collaboration.

In the midst of the invigorating weekend meeting, I found myself immersed in a sea of knowledge and inspiration shared by accomplished Amway team members. Their unwavering optimism and boundless energy were contagious, leaving an impression on me. I was captivated by the caliber of these individuals, their relentless drive, and unwavering determination. It was during those meetings that I experienced a profound realization, a new calling within me, urging me to embrace the path of a business owner. While I cherished my service to the country, the compelling stories and insights offered by the speakers about the joys of entrepreneurship ignited an unquenchable excitement that has not left me to this day.

Quite a few of the speakers also made reference to their faith and they encouraged me to attend a special Sunday morning faith-based service. I had no idea what to expect but I attended with hundreds of other people. By faith I mean religion, but it was presented in a way that was not religious at all. This was a completely foreign concept to me. My family was Catholic but not the church-going type, at least we did not attend church very often. But enough that I understood the very basics of Christianity, and of course I was aware of who Jesus was. But I had never read the Bible. Religion and faith meant nothing to me. But the speaker really made me think.

I don't recall everything the speaker said, or even many of the details, but what he shared shattered my thinking that evening. He told me that Jesus, a man who lived 2,000 years ago, died on a cross for my sins. My sins were many, that much I knew, and I didn't like what my life had become, so I paid careful attention. He told us that Jesus Christ, who was born in Bethlehem, was fully God and fully man, lived a sinless life, died on the cross to bear our sins, and then rose from the grave in order to give us eternal life. I understood this to mean that Jesus saved me from the same sins that were giving me such internal distress. Jesus could give my life purpose. He could absolve me of my sins. He loved me and wanted to be my friend. Inside of me, I could feel that this was good news, and, in fact, the man told me it was THE good news! My spirit lept inside of me.

The ironic thing is that the story of Christianity validated what I already believed about my life. I felt like the speaker could read my mind. He was speaking directly to me. Everything I was thinking and feeling about the emptiness in my soul became very clear to me that morning. The reason I felt so unfulfilled was because of my disconnectedness with God. I was trying to live my life my own way, without any belief in or relationship with God. There was already an internal struggle going on deep inside my soul, but I didn't know how to end it or what to do about it. That's why the story of Jesus made so much sense to me. God the Father was the father I always wanted, and Jesus the friend I always needed.

At the end of the man's message, he specifically asked if anyone in the room wanted to make a public decision to turn his life over to Christ. He asked us to walk to the front of the room to accept Christ, and for prayer. This was also very unexpected. I was mesmerized by the message of Jesus and I looked around the room to see if anyone else was going to stand up for Christ. As I was sitting there my entire life flashed before my eyes. The loneliness I experienced as a child, my troubled relationship with my father, the burdens I carried, and the sinful way I had been living. So, I stood up and ran to the front of the room. I was the first one there, I dropped to my knees, teared-up, and told God I was ready to live for Him. I will never forget the feeling as the Holy Spirit took hold of me. The loneliness was instantly gone. I was now a friend of Jesus and my many sins had been forgiven.

When I returned to the Air Force base later that day, some guys asked if I wanted to join them at the bar. My normal response would have been to join them, and excitedly so. But I was surprised that I had no motivation whatsoever to participate. My sinful nature, as I now understood it, had completely left me. Instead, I grabbed a Bible someone handed me at the meeting and I started to read and study it. I felt compelled to read my Bible and every time I was asked to go to a party, I politely told my airmen friends that I wanted to spend time with God, reading my Bible. As you might imagine, they were surprised, and frankly they didn't take it too well. This wasn't always easy for me so I joined a community of other believers at a local church. This is where and when I discovered the value of fellowship with people who also loved the Lord. From these days on, I was always connected to others in Christ, and it's made all the difference in my life.

When I started this chapter, I told you that I respect you regardless of what you believe or don't believe about God. That's the honest truth. But as you just read, when I met Jesus, my life was completely transformed. I made a bold stand for Christ. I went all in, committing myself to everything the Bible says. Much of today's world is half-hearted. When we deal with a half-hearted world, it can become easy to fall into that half-heartedness. By that I mean you don't take a stand for anything at all. You ride the fence. That's no way to live. The day I ran to the front of the room to ask Jesus to come into my life was the last day I was half-hearted about anything. The result: I'm joyful, content, and bursting with big ideas!

Does this mean I don't have any problems in my life? Does this mean I'm not tempted and sometimes still make mistakes? Does this mean I'm perfect? Of course not. Life is difficult to navigate and I've since experienced many ups and downs over the course of my life, even feelings of depression and anxiety. But the difference is that I'm no longer alone when I face the many challenges in my life. I have someone to go to in prayer, and I have God's Word at my side when I need His guidance and direction. There have been many times in my life when I got on my knees in prayer, for my family, my friends, and for my company. This brings me great peace and comfort, and most importantly, it helps me find solutions and answers. I pray this chapter might also bring you the peace of mind and heart you are yearning for.

❝

"Learn to be humble and give
away as much control as you
can possibly give away.
Trust other people who
want to help you."

❞

7

Trust Is the Glue of Life

I eventually decided to leave Florida for the Washington, D.C. Metro Area, where a friend suggested I replant myself and pursue a career in cybersecurity, which of course I did. I've learned so much since then, both about building a business and about life, and now in this chapter, I delve into what I consider the most crucial principle I've learned throughout my career and life: trust.

As Brian Tracy wisely puts it, "The glue that holds business relationships together is trust, and trust is purely based on integrity." While I concur with this sentiment, I also recognize that trust doesn't always come easily for entrepreneurs. Indeed, trust poses a significant challenge for most entrepreneurs, and it is crucial to address this issue head-on. If we are to nurture and grow our big ideas, we must learn to place our trust in others, just as they place their trust in us. Success thrives on collaborative relationships and cohesive teamwork.

Why do entrepreneurs often struggle to trust others and resist seeking valuable advice? Why do they tend to over-trust themselves while under-trusting their own team members?

I firmly believe that many entrepreneurs find themselves trapped within a self-made bubble. Engrossed in their thoughts and endeavors, they become hypnotized by their own perspectives. Furthermore, the transition from solo-operator to team leader isn't always seamless. During the early stages of a start-up, entrepreneurs often must rely solely on their instincts and ideas, as they may lack external support. Consequently, they become conditioned to making decisions on their own, even when they have a team to rely on.

The danger of dwelling in one's bubble lies in the distorted view of reality it fosters. Trusting solely in oneself leads to a myopic perspective, blinding entrepreneurs to the invaluable contributions that others can provide. Unfortunately, ego-centricity begins to take root, and an unchecked ego can prove detrimental to success. While confidence is an essential trait for driven entrepreneurs, an egotistical and self-centered approach can lead to overconfidence, dismissing facts in favor of their convictions.

The truth is that you can't always be right and you can't possibly understand all the facts. Even when you find yourself in a position of growth and success, don't be fooled into thinking it's all about *me*. Building your own ego will always be contrary to building your company. I highly encourage you to learn to be humble and to give away as much control as you can possibly give away. Let go of your ego and begin to trust other people who want to help you. Those with big egos protect themselves with false pride and refusal to acknowledge information that contradicts them. They are on some level afraid of making mistakes. This can lead them to stick blindly to bad decision making—justifying it anyway they can. They will also impose their self-styled concept of perfectionism onto others, being highly critical and vocal about any weaknesses or mistakes they witness.

I experienced this before I started my company, Agile Cybersecurity Solutions, as an employee of another company (several companies). I saw firsthand how vertical, top-down communication can wreak havoc on an organization and its people. When leadership and management are not open-minded, receptive, available, and have the ability to interact with their people, there's no trust within the organization. When there's no trust, team members don't feel comfortable approaching management with ideas that will solve problems. Unfortunately this is all too common. So often in small companies to large, there is a complete lack of trust in their own people. The founders and the managers they hire work inside their bubbles and expect everyone else to line up and listen without the respect they all deserve.

The bottom line is that if people don't trust that you'll listen to them, they won't talk. But if they do trust you, communication is easy, instant, and effective. You'll move from coordination to collaboration, which is the best kind of communication because it results in success. Without trust, you generate a dysfunctional organization and teams. There is no meaningful connection between people and departments. It's just meaningless coordination. It is trust, and trust alone, that shifts a company into a functional team that gets things done and solves problems.

As you've already read about in this book, my story is full of entrepreneurial ideas and start-ups, even before I became an Amway independent business owner. And for nearly ten years previous to ACS, I worked as an employee in the Cybersecurity industry until I was offered a temporary assignment with Salient, an American private firm that provides analytics and cloud services. I accepted the role but soon transitioned from Salient's subject matter expert and a consultant to a solo start-up entrepreneur. Once again, I ventured out on my own, this time to launch my own cybersecurity company.

I was like a bulldog. My tenacity was unmatched and soon the United States government and private industry hired me to assist with building strong defenses against cyber threats. My business soon boomed, and like many start-up entrepreneurs, I was soon forced into a position where I needed to hire staff. But rather than hire traditional W-2 employees, I went "rogue." I was determined to build an organization that trusted its people. Rather than top-down management which can limit creativity and slow down problem-solving, I went horizontal. I wanted to hire the best cybersecurity professionals in the industry, and then give them the freedom to do their job as they saw best fit. I set my ego aside and refused to make all the decisions at the top. Many process problems are only visible at lower levels, and I wanted to empower faster, better decisions at the lower levels. I also wanted to foster more creativity and better overall communication. With all communication flowing from leaders to team members with little room for dialogue, the top-down approach allows fewer opportunities for creative collaboration.

One challenge with the top-down management approach is that it requires proactive work to keep everyone engaged, connected, and respected. When all decisions are made at the top, the rest of the team might feel that their feedback and opinions aren't valued. I didn't want to create a situation where there was too much distance between myself and the delivery teams working on projects. I did not want to become a clog in the pipeline. So again, I admitted to myself that I was not the only expert in the room. My company would be able to better serve its clients if I trusted my team. I gave them the freedom they deserved to create the solutions our customers demanded.

When I began to search for the best and the brightest people to join my team, I told them that it was OK to fail. When people fail, I want them to reveal the failure sooner than later. Otherwise you end up with a team that plays hide and seek. As a leader you want your team to be honest and transparent with you, so that means you have to accept it when your people fail and not stifle them for it. Work out the problems afterwards and reward them for trying. This is also a part of setting your ego aside. It's not always easy because as the owner, you want everyone to work hard and never make mistakes. But we all do, and it's best to simply acknowledge it upfront. That's what freedom is all about, and freedom in the workplace produces better employees and a better product.

I eventually coined a phrase for my management philosophy. I called it the "ACS Cyber SEAL Program." I found that most of the talent I was seeking could not be hired or trained through traditional means. Good talent doesn't want to be controlled and micromanaged. They want to be trusted. They don't want to report up the chain. Instead they want to be trusted enough to decide how, when, and where to do their work. I went from hiring W-2 employees to finding qualified contractors who I could develop relationships with built on trust. I treated them as my peers, and I discovered that they would integrate seamlessly with existing teams and act as a catalyst for quick and decisive action, critical to next generation cybersecurity services and solutions.

Since I implemented the Cyber SEAL Program, my team has performed exemplary work which has been recognized and rewarded by the highest levels of the United States government. We were once called on to solve a crisis at the Pentagon which more than several hundred staff could not solve. I was once asked to immediately travel to the Middle East, on twenty-four-hours notice, because the Department of Defense needed cybersecurity "boots on the ground" to protect the US Armed Forces. Time and time again our agile team steps up and delivers solutions that even the largest cybersecurity firms cannot. We're fast, creative, and we get the job done.

Trust. My team trusts me. I trust them. Our customers trust us. We trust them as well. Trust is the foundation from which I build my company, and freedom is the flag we wave. The freedom I afford my team is why there is trust. No egos and no bubbles, only belief in each other and the belief that together we can build a safe and more secure environment for our customers.

I will also share that the reason I trust my people is also because I have learned to trust God in every circumstance. Lots of times we go through different trials and following God's plan seems like it doesn't make any sense at all. God is always in control and He will never leave us alone. I shared about my faith in a previous chapter, and I also shared there that I respect your personal beliefs. I happen to be a person of faith, and I integrate my faith into everything I do, even my work in cybersecurity. Maybe that's why *trust* comes easy for me, because I have the fullest confidence that I can trust the Lord in both my personal life and my business.

"The greatest visionaries
throughout history were
often met with disbelief and
resistance before their ideas
revolutionized the world."

8

Embracing the Outlier Inside of You

Are you the kind of person who seems to have a new idea everyday? If so, then you and I both share the same blessing. But as a person blessed with an abundance of fresh ideas, you have undoubtedly faced your fair share of skepticism and criticism. I know that I have. However, remember this: the greatest visionaries throughout history were often met with disbelief and resistance before their ideas revolutionized the world. Embracing your role as an outlier, a disruptor, is a crucial step toward realizing your full creative potential.

In this chapter, I want to share with you what it means to be a BIG idea person by posing three important, clarifying questions. I could probably write an entire book on creativity itself, as it relates to business and entrepreneurship, but in this chapter I simply want to share with you how to embrace you as the outlier.

But first consider for a moment the notion that your creator nature is not a mere coincidence, but a divine gift. In recognizing that you were created by God to create, you tap into a wellspring of inspiration and purpose. Just as the universe constantly expands, so too does your imagination. Embrace this inherent gift and let it guide you toward uncharted territories, for you are an instrument of God-given ingenuity. At the same time, also remember that not everyone understands your restless energy of a creator. The very concept of constantly venturing into new directions can be perplexing to those rooted in familiarity and tradition. Be patient with those who doubt you. The misunderstanding of others is not a reflection of your capabilities, but a testament to the uniqueness of your visionary spirit. Embrace it and be a BIG idea person!

My First Question:
What Does It Mean to Be a BIG Idea Person?

Being a BIG idea person goes beyond simply generating a few novel concepts. Instead, it embodies a mindset that constantly seeks to push boundaries, challenge conventions, and revolutionize the way we perceive and interact with the world. A BIG idea person possesses a unique ability to think expansively and envision possibilities where others see limitations.

At the heart of being a BIG idea person is a refusal to accept the status quo. While others may be content with incremental improvements, you strive to envision solutions and opportunities that go beyond existing frameworks. You possess the audacity to question long-established norms because you understand that true innovation lies beyond the confines of familiarity. Does this sound like you? If so, then you're a BIG idea person.

Let me offer a personal example. When I founded ACS, I was discontent with how most companies approached their work. The work environments demonstrated a noticeable lack of collaboration and an inclination toward working in isolation rather than fostering a sense of collective effort. Moreover, their organizations exhibited an excessive adherence to bureaucratic procedures, resulting in a rigid and cumbersome decision-making process. As a result, they were slow to act and failed to find creative solutions to problems. Frankly, the company I was working for before I founded ACS regularly shut down new ideas altogether. So as a BIG idea person, I envisioned a different kind of company, one that valued creativity and innovation, and not simply solid technology. Yes, good technology is absolutely critical. But so are the ideas behind the technology. So, I refused to accept the status quo. I wanted to push the boundaries in how I approached cybersecurity. The result of my BIG idea attitude is my company today, a product and vendor agnostic deliverer of elite cybersecurity services and solutions.

If you're going to be a BIG idea person, I encourage you to never stop pushing the boundaries. Don't take "no" for an answer and don't let anyone tell you that "this is just the way we do things." The biggest and best ideas often come when and where you least expect it. But you have to look for the opportunities and be prepared to embrace them, in spite of any resistance you may face. Imagine a future that is radically different from the present and then chart a course to turn that vision into reality. Believe in yourself and your ideas. This unwavering belief in the power of your ideas fuels your drive to overcome obstacles and inspire others to rally behind your vision.

Also, always lean into your intuition. I believe that Experience + Intuition = Creativity and Solutions. Intuition, often described as a gut feeling or inner knowing, is a subconscious cognitive process that provides us with insights beyond logical reasoning. It taps into our past experiences, knowledge, and emotions, and guides us toward instant understanding without the need for conscious analysis. By tapping into this inner wisdom, we gain access to a vast reservoir of untapped potential. I tend to believe that God is the source of my intuition. You might as well make decisions based not simply on math and facts, but on creativity and intuition. This has always worked for me.

My Second Question: How Do You Cultivate Creativity and Curiosity?

I liken the creative process to a piano or violin which needs to be tuned. In a similar way to how musicians need to regularly tune their instruments, your creative ecosystem demands deliberate attention. If you're going to be a BIG idea person, you have to continually cultivate it.

I tell people that in order to cultivate a creative approach to your work, you must have a science fiction mindset. One of my favorite science fiction movies is Minority Report, starring Tom Cruise, because it has striking parallels with the journey of becoming a creative person. In the movie, "pre-crime" represents a system that predicts crimes before they happen, essentially eliminating the element of choice and personal agency. Similarly, many aspiring creatives find themselves trapped within the confines of conventional thinking. But just as the protagonist, John Anderton (Tom Cruise), breaks free from the shackles of pre-crime, embracing his own unique path, we too must dare to challenge the status quo and embrace our creative impulses.

It's also important to surround yourself with individuals who understand and appreciate your innate desire for novelty. Seek out fellow creators, mentors, and collaborators who can support and challenge you in equal measure. Cultivate an environment that nourishes your ideas.

It may come as a surprise to you, but within my world-class team of cybersecurity professionals, I've assembled a diverse group consisting of not only top-notch experts with technical pedigrees but also individuals with artistic and musical backgrounds. I even have a concert pianist on my team. Recognizing the importance of a well-rounded team, I firmly believe that incorporating individuals with creative expertise is essential. Their unique perspectives and imaginative approaches adds creativity in a way that enables us to tackle challenges from unconventional angles. By embracing this diverse array of talents, we establish a foundation that allows us to push the boundaries of cybersecurity and uncover innovative solutions that may have otherwise remained undiscovered. I believe that good science and good math demand good creativity, so I've always surrounded myself with creative people. As a BIG idea person, I encourage you to do the same. It doesn't matter what industry or sector you work in, creativity is key.

Another important way I nurture my creativity is by shifting my work environments. Change in the work environment introduces novelty, stimulating our senses and sparking curiosity. By deliberately seeking out new surroundings, we expose ourselves to fresh stimuli, disrupting established routines and thought patterns. This shift in perspective creates fertile ground for innovative thinking, as our minds adapt to various situations and are compelled to explore alternative approaches to problem-solving. Long periods in a static work environment can lead to complacency and stagnant thinking. By changing our work environment often, we inject an element of surprise and disruption into our routine.

This is why I travel often, even to far-off places like Portugal. Sometimes I work near a beach, other times in or near the mountains. In fact, my home is not far from the beautiful Shenandoah mountains. This breaks the monotony and all discomfort and uncertainty that comes along with work. It revitalizes my creative faculties and pushes me beyond our comfort zones. Sometimes when I travel and work, I observe my surroundings and ask myself questions about the people around me. For example, when I work from my home in West Palm Beach, Florida, I observe the wealth and success that so many people there have discovered and accumulated. So I ask myself, "How did they accomplish such great things?" This inspires me to be more creative in my work, so that I also can become more successful in my work.

Finally, My Third Question: How Do You Turn Ideas into Action?

While generating BIG ideas is a remarkable feat, a BIG idea person recognizes that execution is equally vital. You have to possess the ability to translate your vision into actionable plans, break down complex challenges into manageable steps, and rally a team to bring your ideas to fruition. I believe that execution is the step many creative people don't fully comprehend. Many great ideas are never fulfilled or realized because of poor execution. While the generation of innovative concepts is essential, true impact and transformation lie in their execution.

I think many times people get overwhelmed or intimidated when they get past the ideation stage and begin to execute. I certainly had some fear and trepidation when I first launched my cybersecurity company. But I quickly learned that by breaking down the execution process into manageable and actionable goals, I was less intimidated. Large, ambitious ideas can be overwhelming, but by breaking them down into smaller, achievable milestones, you create a sense of progress and momentum. Each milestone becomes a stepping stone toward the ultimate realization of your vision. Focus on achievable steps, celebrate small victories, and build confidence along the journey. This is what strategic planning is all about.

Execution begins with strategic planning—a deliberate and well-thought-out roadmap for transforming ideas into tangible outcomes. A clear vision, concrete objectives, and actionable steps are essential components of an effective execution plan. By carefully mapping out the path ahead, identifying potential challenges, and devising strategies to overcome them, you set the stage for a successful execution. It also involves the judicious allocation of resources, which means you identify the necessary personnel, financial support, technology, and other resources needed to bring your idea to fruition. Mobilize and leverage these resources effectively, ensuring that the right people with the appropriate skills and expertise are involved. Strategic planning is a big topic and if you haven't explored it for yourself, I encourage you to take a deep dive. Your great ideas will remain just great ideas if you don't master the art of strategic planning.

Of course, great ideas thrive in an environment of collaboration and open communication. I've shared this throughout this book. You should always strive to foster a culture of teamwork, where individuals are encouraged to contribute their unique perspectives, skills, and experiences. Effective communication channels ensure that everyone is aligned, informed, and empowered to execute their roles effectively. Regular feedback and open dialogue facilitate the seamless flow of information, enabling swift decision-making and agile execution. It truly is all about being agile, and when you establish a culture of ownership, where individuals take pride in their contributions and are committed to collective success, your organization will always be agile. Agility is the key to the successful execution of great ideas.

Be Flexible and Adaptive

The bottom line is that the execution of great ideas is rarely a linear path. Embrace adaptability and be prepared to refine your approach along the way. As you navigate unforeseen challenges and gather feedback, be open to adjusting your strategies and tactics. Learn from failures, and I promise you will have many of them! Embracing the iterative process empowers you to pivot when necessary and ultimately enhances the quality of execution.

As you create and develop your BIG ideas, you also want to make sure that every idea aligns with your fundamentals. For me, that means my faith and what I read in my Bible. Every idea has to align with my God-given calling and talents before I even begin to think about execution. Whatever your foundation is, it's vitally important you keep it front and center and you be creative and executive. Otherwise you will end up chasing rabbits and later regret your decisions.

Let me offer you a real-life example. My company is frequently offered the opportunity to re-sell cyber-security products. These are ready-made, turnkey programs that I could, in theory, buy and then resell for a profit. In some ways this is "easy money" and an attractive way to grow my business. On occasion I liked the idea so I embraced it, but then later I regretted my decision because the products themselves didn't always work, which made my company look bad. I admit it was a bad decision on my part, and I also admit that I did not think about (and pray about) whether or not it aligned with my core values. If I had done so, I wouldn't have made the mistake in the first place. Fortunately, I learned my lesson early-on and today we deploy our own custom solutions that we stand-by and believe in. The Bible says, "For those who seek after riches and gaining them quickly, their appetite will never be satisfied. The root of these desires is greed and the pursuit for more will never end" (Ecclesiastes 5:10). Take some time to look inward and decide who you are and what you believe in, then build your ideas around your core values.

This chapter contains so much information, you could probably spend weeks or even years studying about everything I've shared. But my intention here is not to include anything and everything, but instead to inspire you to begin the process of becoming a person of BIG ideas. I believe you have been chosen to think big, create big ideas, and take action. We are ALL chosen. I commission you to go find your BIG idea. I believe in you!

"By confronting our fears head-on, we liberate ourselves from the constraints of comfort zones, unlocking the true extent of our capabilities."

9

Transition Strategies:
Embracing Change and
Empowering Growth

The idea of an "exit strategy" has long been a topic of discussion in the business community. I'm frequently asked what my exit strategy is, and in fact I sometimes receive inquiries and even offers from other venture capitalists to acquire my business. Do I engage in dialogue with them? Sometimes, but only to learn more about the industry and my competitors. I don't intend to sell my company because I love my work and I have no intention of exiting what I love doing.

Someday I may decide to sell my company but that possibility is certainly not on my horizon. But even if I do sell, I won't exit. "What do you mean by that, Carlos?" you might ask.

Before I give you my answer, what is meant by an exit strategy? An exit strategy often refers to a plan or set of actions devised by an entrepreneur or investor to disengage from a particular business venture. The purpose is to maximize financial returns, mitigate risks, or there might be many other purposes an owner wants to sell. It also outlines the steps and conditions under which the individual or entity intends to exit the venture, which could include selling off assets, liquidating holdings, merging with another company, or even going public through an initial public offering (IPO). An exit strategy provides a structured approach to transition out of the venture while optimizing the value created during its duration.

While all of this makes sense, as a visionary entrepreneur, I challenge the traditional notion of exit strategies and propose a revolutionary approach—transition strategies. In this chapter, I want to share with you how I've redefined the way I view change and transition in both my work and in my life. Prepare to shatter the conventional mindset and embrace the power of transition strategies to leverage experience and strengths for lasting success. I encourage you to stop thinking about an exit and instead think about a transition.

To understand the essence of a transition strategy, let's explore what an exit strategy often looks like to most people. Traditionally, I have found that exiting often implies disengagement and even a hasty escape from a venture or endeavor. It suggests abandoning all the valuable experience and knowledge accumulated during the journey. I refer to it not as existing but running away, much like you'd run away from a bull. They still run bulls on the Portuguese Island of Terceira, which date all the way back to the sixteenth century. I've never participated but each summer hundreds of brave villagers dress in white and wave their jackets and blankets as the bulls spring forward, horns primed, and charge. Each villager plays this dangerous game until he (or she) skips away safely to the applause of the crowd.

When confronted by a real bull, indeed your goal should be to exit! But rarely is work and life a bull run, yet oftentimes people think about it as such. When they come face to face with the bull, they panic and seek the fastest way out.

Exiting a business or venture is often influenced by several factors, ranging from personal to external circumstances including financial challenges when a business is experiencing financial difficulties or facing mounting debts. Burnout can also play a key role as running a business can be demanding and stressful. Somtimes personal circumstances or shifting prior-ities, such as family commitments, health issues, or other life events, can prompt business owners to prioritize other aspects of their lives and make an exit (this is of course understandable, and sometimes does require a resignation and exit). Other times internal

conflicts within the management team or among business partners can create a toxic environment, leading
some individuals to exit hastily to escape the stress and
tension, or pressure from investors, stakeholders, or
external advisors to exit the business due to specific
market conditions or perceived strategic opportunities
can also contribute to hasty decisions.

While many or even all of these given reasons to
exit, I believe in most cases they are impulsive decisions. In many cases, entrepreneurs make hasty exit
decisions based on emotions, impulsive reactions to
challenges, or a lack of clear planning and analysis. So
they run from the bull and jump over the fence. The
problem is that this approach limits our potential for
growth and hampers our ability to capitalize on hard-
earned expertise. Transition strategies, on the other
hand, herald a new era of empowerment and transformation. By embracing transitions, we open doors
to endless possibilities, allowing us to gracefully pivot
and evolve. Rather than abandoning our achievements,
we should leverage our experiences and strengths as a
stepping stone toward the next chapter of our journey.
Transitions propel us forward, enabling us to tran-
scend limitations and explore new horizons.

As you've read my story, you've seen how many
times I've successfully transitioned during my life. I
transitioned from a young immigrant boy on the

streets of New Jersey to budding entreprenuer on the beaches of Florida, from a struggling student to an honor student at the Virginia Military Institute (VMI) and to an officer in the United States Air Force. Then I transitioned from military service to a successful sales and marketing career as an Amway independent business owner, to a limousine driver of the rich and famous, and eventually to Washington, D.C., where I transitioned my way through the world of cybersecurity to where I stand today as the Founder and CEO of my own cybersecurity company, ACS. Did I ever quit? Not once. Did I exit? Not once. I embraced my experiences and moved in a new direction, always after deep thought and prayer. I didn't "jump ship" in desperation. But rather I continued to work hard and be diligent until it was time to transition to my next calling.

Formulating a transition strategy demands a blend of self-awareness, foresight, and adaptability. It's important to understand your motivations for change and to recognize the untapped potential within you. We all have untapped potential. But if you run away from what you're doing, you may never find it. So by working to align your passions, your skills, and your aspirations, you create a roadmap that channels your accumulated knowledge into a fresh and purposeful direction. The transition strategy becomes a blueprint for growth, paving the way for success in uncharted territories.

It's not always easy, I readily admit. Transitioning necessitates courage—the courage to embrace change and embrace the unknown. It is not a journey for the faint-hearted, but for the bold and ambitious dreamers who dare to challenge the status quo. By confronting our fears head-on, we liberate ourselves from the constraints of comfort zones, unlocking the true extent of our capabilities. Have there been times when fear and panic rose up within me? Certainly. I wouldn't be human otherwise. But I've pressed on despite the fear, and I refused to simply leave it all behind and then aimlessly do something totally different. In fact, when you look at my journey, you might think my trek was haphazard. On the contrary, I learned what I could at each stage of my life and career, and then took my experiences with me when I moved on to the next stage. That's far from an exit strategy. That's a transition strategy.

Transition is all about leveraging our experience and strengths. Instead of abandoning our past endeavors, try to view them as building blocks that fortify your foundation. Identify transferable skills and knowledge that are applicable in your new pursuits. By harnessing these assets, you will also gain a competitive advantage, ensuring that your journey of transition is founded on a bedrock of wisdom. Yes, transitioning comes with its share of challenges and uncertainties. The easy path is to exit. But as you traverse uncharted territory, resilience becomes your ally. The ability to bounce back from setbacks and maintain unwavering determination is the hallmark of a transition strategist. So embrace the bumps in the road and view them as opportunities!

Let me also share the importance of understanding "why" you're doing what you're doing. When you have a deep understanding and self-awareness of your internal clock, you're going to be a better time-keeper. You will intuitively know better when it's time to transition, and how to transition. The best entrepreneurs have a strong foundation and a sense of core purpose. For me, I consider myself to be an active participant in the American experiment.

For an entrepreneur to be an active participant in the American experiment means embracing and embodying the core principles that define the essence of the United States and its democratic ideals. The American experiment symbolizes the Founding Fathers and the ongoing quest to form a more perfect union, where individuals are empowered to pursue life, liberty, and the pursuit of happiness.

I believe that entrepreneurs are the driving force behind all innovation and creativity, constantly pushing the boundaries of what is possible. They embody the spirit of the American experiment by fostering an environment where new ideas, technologies, and solutions emerge, contributing to the nation's progress and prosperity. Also, just as the Founding Fathers risked so much for the freedoms we possess as Americans today, the American experiment celebrates risk-taking and resilience. Entrepreneurs like myself, and like you, embrace uncertainty and persevere through challenges, embodying the belief that success can be achieved through hard work, determination, and the ability to learn from failure. This is largely what inspires me to keep going strong.

In essence, an entrepreneur being an active participant in the American experiment goes beyond the pursuit of personal success; it involves aligning their business endeavors with the values and principles that underpin the nation's foundation. By embodying these core ideals, entrepreneurs contribute to the ongoing narrative of the American dream and play a vital role in shaping a future that reflects the values of liberty, opportunity, and progress. For me, this gives me a strong purpose and it prevents me from making a quick exit. It guides me through my transitions as I seek to better myself, my family, and my community.

This particular chapter was written from my home in Portugal where I can see both the beautiful ocean on one side and rolling farms on the other. I can't help but wonder what would have happened if I never came to America. Might I be a farmer on those hills? Maybe so, and I might have lived a full and happy life. But I would never have experienced the freedom that I have as an American. I likely would not have found a way to transition my life and work in a way that is fulfilling and so rewarding. Portugal and many other countries around the world, while all good places, don't reward freedom the way we do in America. I'm so grateful to God for granting me this opportunity, and especially for the opportunity to defend capitalism and democracy through my work in cybersecurity. I count it all a blessing and while I cherish my homeland and love the people there, I pray they may also someday feel the freedom that I feel, so that they also may transition and not exit.

My friend, dig deep and find your purpose. Decide *why* you're an entrepreneur and then take it by force. Face your bull. Don't allow temporary fears to become permanent decisions that distract you from your true calling in life. I promise it will make your road easier and the load lighter. And always remember the words of Adam Smith who inspired our system of capitalism, "The real tragedy of the poor is the poverty of their aspirations."

"The spirit of entrepreneurship leads to a more dynamic economy, fostering a climate of freedom where new ideas can flourish."

10

I Believe in Free Enterprise

Wherever I go, people ask me why I'm such a strong proponent of capitalism. Yes, you could definitely say that I'm pro-freedom, pro-capitalism, and pro-America. But it's not just me. Many immigrants agree with me, and, in fact, I would say that a vast majority agree with me. For most immigrants, the word "socialism" is a word that evokes a weakened work ethic, stifled innovation, and excessive reliance on the government. When an immigrant arrives in the United States, the idea that they can suddenly create their own life, on their own terms, comes alive. It's exciting to discover for the first time that you can be your own boss and have the freedom to determine your own destiny. It's also exciting to learn that the United States of America encourages innovation, ingenuity, and entrepreneurism, as opposed to so many other countries where it's discouraged or even outright banned.

Did you know that some of America's most successful entrepreneurs are immigrants?

Phil Libin, the founder of Evernote, is an immigrant from Russia. Levi Straus came from Germany. Sergey Brin, cofounder of Google was also born in Russia. Jan Koum who created WhatsApp is from Ukraine. Intel's original CEO is Andy Grove, who is an immigrant from Budapest. Pierre Omidyar who founded eBay was born in Iran. Instagram's cofounder, Mike Krieger, is an immigrant from Brazil. The list goes on and on!

Are you surprised? As an expat myself, I've gained a perspective about free enterprise and immigration that others may not have had the opportunity to develop. The narrative of immigrants becoming successful entrepreneurs may sound like a fable of the American Dream. Some may even call it "fake news". However, the statistics back me up on this:

- One in four American entrepreneurs are immigrants, a number that has increased dramatically over the past decades.

- Nearly half of all businesses that were founded in the last thirty years have an immigrant involved in their founding.

- Of the 2017 Fortune 500 list companies, nearly half were founded by immigrants or their children.

When I travel to Portugal, which is still a socialist society, I observe a certain sense of hopelessness among many of the people. Portugal is still a young democracy, so some of the despair comes from the memory of the regime that ruled Portugal from 1926 to 1974. It still remains fresh in many people's minds. But even still, many people in Portugal are still in bondage to the idea of socialism. When I talk to the Portuguese about free enterprise, many tell me they worry that more capitalism will lead to more inequality in Portuguese society.

Some will argue with me that Portugal is not a socialist society. Yes, there can be many nuances in the economic and social systems of different countries, and labels like "socialist" or "capitalist" do not fully capture the complexity of their socio-economic structures. In the case of Portugal, some people describe it as a social democracy, where a mixed economy coexists with a strong emphasis on social welfare and economic regulation, rather than a purely socialist society. I don't entirely agree. While a significant amount of the economy is privately held, all essential services like education and healthcare are publicly owned, exhibiting the characteristics of socialist systems. Also, government regulation on private business is significant and a great burden for business owners. Portugal has a very high corporate tax rate of up to 31.5 percent, and companies are severely limited in the amount of net operating losses they can use to offset future profits. Unlike in the United States, they are unable to use losses to reduce past taxable income. Can you imagine that? This makes it an uphill battle for every entrepreneur.

Oftentimes when I visit my homeland, others will ask me about capitalism and free enterprise. They want to learn more about how to start and grow a business. They are hungry for information and resources. I tell them that free enterprise is the only path to true economic freedom and prosperity. Economist Milton Freidman once wrote, "So that the record of history is absolutely crystal clear that there is no alternative way, so far discovered, of improving the lot of the ordinary people that can hold a candle to the productive activities that are unleashed by a free-enterprise system." Portugal is an example of this. I'm proud of my birthplace and its people. I'm proud that they've come this far, but I also want to help them understand how capitalism can work for them, and not against them.

As an immigrant who takes great pride in how democracy and free enterprise has improved my life, I've taken time to study America's founding documents.

I venture to say that I've spent more time studying them than most American citizens who were born here. The reason I believe in capitalism and free enterprise is because I believe I was created by God and in His image. The Founders of the American Revolution also rejected those who believed we were created apart from God. As the Declaration of Independence states, all men "are endowed by their Creator with certain unalienable rights."

When you believe and embrace this, you also discover that freedom should be protected and fought for at all costs. All men and women desire to be free. It's how God made us. Extreme taxation, excessive controls, oppressive government competition with business, frustrated minorities, and forgotten Americans are not the products of free enterprise. They are the residue of centralized bureaucracy, of politicians and rulers who don't believe that God made us for freedom, but rather for bondage. The essential difference between the visions of socialists and capitalists is that "We the People" tell the government what to do, the government does not tell the people what to do. Why? Because we serve God and not a bureaucracy.

But also, beyond the philosophical reasons, I'm a proponent of free enterprise. I believe that economic independence motivates people to live happier, more productive lives. It gives them the freedom to pursue their passions, make their own decisions, and control their financial destiny. It drives innovation and progress because entrepreneurs are often the driving force behind innovation and progress in society. By identifying gaps in the market and developing new products, services, or technologies, entrepreneurs contribute to economic growth and societal advancement. This spirit of entrepreneurship leads to a more dynamic and adaptable economy, fostering a climate of freedom where new ideas can flourish. My company drives innovation in the area of cybersecurity. We solve problems for the government and industry, and as a result my team members are able to advance their own careers, earning more money and thereby putting them in a stronger position to support their families.

Free enterprise also drives individual autonomy. As entrepreneurs build their businesses, they have the freedom to shape their own destinies and make decisions that align with their personal values and goals. They have the ability to choose their own work schedule, determine their company culture, and pursue projects that they are passionate about. This level of individual autonomy allows entrepreneurs to create a sense of freedom and fulfillment in their professional lives. There's not a better feeling in the world to wake up each morning and be in control of your day. That's free enterprise at work. This is partly why I created the Cyber SEAL Program, so that each of my team members can have the autonomy they deserve.

Entrepreneurs are significant job creators, and the ability to provide employment opportunities to others is a crucial aspect of freedom. By starting and expanding businesses, entrepreneurs not only create jobs for themselves but also for others in their communities. This has a positive impact on economic growth, reduces unemployment, and provides individuals with the freedom to choose meaningful work and support their families. I personally take great pride in being able to employ men and women who are able to support their families and do things they love as a result of my company.

Finally, I believe that entrepreneurship can be a powerful tool for social mobility, enabling individuals from diverse backgrounds to rise above their circumstances and achieve success. Unlike traditional career paths that may be constrained by factors like education, connections, or socioeconomic status, entrepreneurship allows individuals to create their own opportunities and overcome systemic barriers. This promotes a more inclusive and equitable society, where freedom is not limited by one's background but rather by their creativity, perseverance, and hard work. Of course, I am a testament to this, as an immigrant who comes from very meager means. But because of freedom and capitalism, I was able to rise above it and create wealth for my family. This would have been almost impossible if I had been raised in Portugal.

Let me offer one more BIG idea that I've discovered along the way, and that's the idea of short-term thinking and long-term thinking. I believe that a free-enterprise system inspires people to plan for the long-term. When you own a business you have to think beyond today. You have payroll to meet and bills to pay. If you only think about today's needs, you'll go out of business. I've never met a successful entrepreneur who doesn't think and plan for next week, next month, and next year. Conversely, socialist societies have less cause to think long-term. They are concerned mostly with the present, putting food on the table today. That's because there aren't as many "owners" in the culture. People expect the government to serve all their needs. They don't care about how or when, they simply demand it happen now. The consequences of this short-term thinking is less innovation, less ingenuity, and less productivity.

Over time a "we want it now" culture begins to weaken and become more dependent on a government that cannot generate the funds it needs to meet the demand of their citizens. So this is why I also believe so strongly in the free-enterprise system. I believe it's God-inspired because God is not a short-term thinker either. He desires for all of us to think about tomorrow!

The essence of freedom is free enterprise. We need to fuel it. Over time people feel beat-up if they have no hope. Only free enterprise fuels hope. Big government limits your potential. Big corporations also limit your potential. Only entrepreneurism provides individuals with the freedom to take control of their economic destinies, pursue their passions, make independent decisions, create jobs, and contribute to the progress of society. By fostering a culture of entrepreneurship, we promote freedom and empower individuals to shape their lives and make a positive impact on the world.